THE GREAT KOALA SCAM

GREEN PROPAGANDA, JUNK SCIENCE,
GOVERNMENT WASTE & CRUELTY TO ANIMALS

Vic Jurskis

Connor Court Publishing

CONNOR COURT PUBLISHING PTY LTD
PO Box 7257
Redland Bay QLD 4165
sales@connorcourt.com
www.connorcourt.com

Front cover: A reserve on Raymond Island. Lack of mild burning has led to tree decline, irruption of koalas and growth of dense scrub or bracken.

Back cover: A hungry koala in a chronically declining tree on Raymond Island. Any tender new shoots which escape being eaten by koalas are, later on, attacked by insects adapted to eating harder foliage.

Photos by the Author

ISBN: 978-1-925826-79-1 (pbk.)

Cover design by Maria Giordano

Printed in Australia

CONTENTS

FOREWORD

I grew up with koalas on Phillip Island, Victoria. In the late 1940s and early 1950s the occasional koala would wander through the township of Newhaven, stop briefly at a suitable tree and then move on. I knew nothing about them except that Phillip Island was considered something special because leaves of *Eucalyptus viminalis* were the preferred food for koalas and this was the dominant tree of residual woodlands and roadside vegetation where koalas were abundant. Later I learnt a little about the range of individual koalas and that they were capable of moving quite long distances in a short time—but not much more.

I was delighted when Vic asked me to review his manuscript. I learnt a lot about the history, distribution and ecology of koalas in Australia and it reminded me that the role of fire in the ecology of Australian animals is a neglected science. I was dismayed, but not surprised, that his paper on the ecological history of koalas was rejected by the scientific community because his conclusions were contrary to the popular view of scientists in that field and people with vested interests in koala management.

Vic is not the first scientist to have had their findings rejected out of hand by their colleagues without debate. I had a paper, which introduced a new factor to predicting fire behaviour, rejected by reviewers with the comment *"This cannot be right because, if it is, it invalidates the last 40 years of fire research"*. Fortunately, I convinced the editor that this comment alone justified publication to raise debate and encourage others to repeat the research. Once accepted, the role of headfire shape and width in determining fire spread became obvious and is now a major consideration to protect firefighters from entrapment.

Others have been fired, not because their findings were proven wrong, but because rejection of the established view violated the "*code of conduct*" of the organisation. Increasingly scientists are asked to sign confidentiality agreements so that criticism of the science is suppressed. Vic is, perhaps, the first to provide a detailed account of discussions with editors and reviewers. I trust that readers will evaluate the evidence that he puts to support his conclusions, and review the previously hidden debate with editors and peers. And if they are sceptical, which is not a bad thing, take the time to examine the material and references he has provided, and consider the importance of scientific debate.

N. P. Cheney PSM

Fellow Institute of Foresters of Australia

Project Leader CSIRO Bushfire Behaviour and Management 1975 -2001

Recipient: The CSIRO Medal for Research Achievement 2003,

The International Association of Wildland Fire 2010 Ember Award for outstanding achievement in wildland fire science

DEDICATION

This book is dedicated to the memory of Athol Hodgson AM, 1930-2018. Athol grew up in the bush and graduated as a Forester from Melbourne University about the time I was born. In 1962 he became a Fire Research Officer and was soon awarded a Churchill Fellowship to study in North America. In 1968, Athol published an article in the American *Journal of Forestry* explaining the basis of *Control Burning in Eucalypt Forests*[1]:

> *Doubling the available fuel usually doubles the rate of spread of the fire and increases its intensity fourfold. Control is made extremely difficult by mass short-distance spotting from stringybark fuel and spectacular long-distance spotting from candlebark fuels. Control burning over large areas ... cheaply and effectively reduces the incidence of high intensity wildfires and minimizes damage.*

Since then, modern land and fire managers have found that burning not only minimises wildfire damage, but actually improves the environment and enhances biodiversity. Fairdinkum science supports Traditional Aboriginal Knowledge that frequent mild burning is the only way to maintain a healthy and safe landscape.

Athol Hodgson was a driving force for pragmatic, scientific fire management in *Forests Commission Victoria*. He reached the rank of Commissioner in 1983, just as academics with no experience of burning, but lots of silly theories, were looking for reasons to disallow it. After the Commission was disbanded, he became Chief Fire Officer of the *Department of Conservation Forests and Lands* until he 'retired' in 1987.

It is a sad indictment of our society that Athol's achievements have been negated by green academics, bureaucrats and politicians of the wilderness cult. But Athol *took up arms against the slings and arrows*. After our Nation was charred and our Capital devastated in 2003, he gave evidence to the Nairn Inquiry which once again came up with the solution to our self-inflicted problems.[2] Unfortunately his successors joined their counterparts in NSW and swept it under the carpet using the COAG report.[3] Athol persisted in the *good fight* through the *Stretton Group*, and set up *Forest Fire Victoria*. He never gave up.

I would have given up long ago if not for the inspiration provided by Athol and a few others like him. In 2015 he gladdened my heart with the following email message:

> **Subject:** *FIRESTICK ECOLOGY*
>
> *Hi Vic.*
> *Thank you for autographing a copy of your book and giving me the best two reads I've had since I read Scouting for Boys by Robert Baden Powell about 70 long years ago.*
> *Yes I've read it twice. I've also bought 6 copies and will send them where they might do some good. ...*
>
> *Congratulations and best wishes*
> *Athol*

Unfortunately, they've done no good so far, but thanks to Athol, I'll keep trying.

Notes

1   Hodgson 1968
2   House of Representatives Select Committee 2003
3   Jurskis 2015 pp.173-176

INTRODUCTION

Good news doesn't boost TV ratings, sell newspapers or aid fundraising campaigns, but there is a huge industry based on seemingly concocted environmental crises. Multinational green 'charities' such as *World Wildlife Fund* might collapse if the simple truth got out. That's why I want to tell you about koalas.

I didn't think I'd need to write this book because I naively trusted in scientific debate. My *Ecological History of the Koala* was accepted for publication in CSIRO's *Wildlife Research* journal. That should have been enough to start a debate, particularly after it was publicised in *The Australian* and I was interviewed by Fran Kelly on *ABC Radio National*. There was a brief flurry of debate involving some scientists, but no scientific debate.

For example, Professor Frank Carrick AM apparently lodged an official protest with *ABC RN*'s executive producer. Carrick is the *Koala Study Program Chief Investigator* at The University of Queensland. He said that he was outraged by the misrepresentation of the status of koalas, and that *"there is substantial consensus amongst Ecologists with significant knowledge as to the dire severity and underlying causes"* [of recent population crashes].[1]

Carrick went on: *"I don't believe it* [my paper] *really contains a basis for the more egregious sweeping generalisations promulgated in the interview"*. (I looked in a dictionary and found that egregious means outstandingly bad. I'm not sure what *more egregious* means.) According to Carrick *"the challenge to conventional wisdom is not based on objective reality!"* and *"is just ludicrous—at least 80% of Koala habitat in existence at the time of European occupation has been destroyed"*.

In 1988, Professor Carrick produced a map[2] showing the *"approximate likely distribution of koalas 200 years ago"*—a time when Europeans didn't know they existed. Carrick had them right across most of eastern Australia. By contrast, award-winning historian Bill Gammage says *"their locations were distinct, lightly populated and few"*.[3] Professor Carrick recently told a Senate Inquiry into *Australia's Extinction Crisis*, koalas were so scarce 40 years ago, when he started studying them at University of NSW, that he had to use *"surplus"* koalas from Victoria *"and the decline has accelerated in the last decade"*. I guess he may have some sort of mental block about the irruptions that occurred in-between.

The *good professor* dismissed my allegedly *"eccentric view"* as *"completely fallacious denial"* and stated that *"RN Breakfast has ... orchestrated music to the ears of vested interests who wish to continue the unfettered, ongoing destruction of Australia's residual forests and woodlands"*.[1] I guarantee you that I have no vested interest, only a passionate desire to reinstate the beautiful, healthy, safe and diverse landscape that I was privileged to experience in my youth.

Unlike *RN Breakfast*, *The Australian* responded to the professor's outrage with two follow-up articles. Carrick likened my paper to *"climate-change denial"* and rejected it as a *"significant departure from reality"*. Environment Editor Graham Lloyd produced a colourful article covering the best part of a page—*KOALAS IN FREE FALL*. He pronounced that *"historical records disagree"* with me, because millions of koalas were killed *"at the beginning of the 20th century"*. Lloyd seems happy to deny the documented scarcity of koalas during the first 100 years of European occupation. He described me as a *sceptic* [i.e. a scientist] and quoted me eight times, but hasn't spoken with me or responded to my communications.

Lloyd's story featured a half-page photo of a female koala and her joey, seemingly posed on top of a windrow of dead trees. She didn't look very comfortable sitting with her bum on a log and hanging on to a branch stub with her hands and the first toe of each foot (the one with no claw). Nor did the joey look happy, or even natural, sitting and reaching out for mum's arm. Dead trees had been pushed and stacked, but the caption described this apparent clearing operation as "*logging ... near Kin Kin*".

Scientists from *Australian Koala Foundation*, *National Parks Association*, *World Wildlife Fund* etc., were quoted to back up the story. I've 'agreed them to death' about the recent population crashes, and explained that they're inevitable consequences of irruptions. Lloyd also referred to Sue Arnold from *Australians for Animals* who managed to convince US authorities to list koalas under their Endangered Species Act. Arnold said estimates of koala numbers are "*highly questionable*". I fully agree with her. It doesn't matter, because koalas were naturally very scarce.

Arnold had stated on her *Koala Crisis* facebook site[4]:

> *After the headline in the Australian on Saturday – 'The Great Koala Scam': falling numbers not a crisis, says expert – quoting well known anti environmentalist fanatic, Vic Jurskis, was followed up on Monday with ABC's Fran Kelly interviewing this horrible excuse for an ecologist.* sic
>
> *... This same nasty biased man writes that Queensland State Environment Minister Steven Miles plan (last year) to set up a "brains trust" on koalas "is a plan to ban dogs from a couple of suburbs where they are currently feeding on starving, diseased koalas living in declining backyard trees".*

Arnold reckoned that I "*raved on*" and that my "*ignorance*" was worthy of an Olympic Gold Medal. Also: "*Jurskis is a forester who hates conservationists*".[4] However, her comments were quite moderate compared to some feedback I received via 'social' media from a Wildlife Carer called Jae Price: "*If your the same Vic Jurskis as in the Australian paper. Them you pal are a complete fucwit with your head jammed up your arse. If it's not the same block then I apologize.*" sic Anyway, I was pleased to have received some publicity and anticipated that some scientific debate would ensue.

Unfortunately, this was not to be the case. You'd think that Professor Carrick and his like-minded colleagues would jump at the opportunity to submit a response to my "*ideology*" in *Wildlife Research*[5], and 'set the record straight'. But that's not how 'scientific consensus' works. The groupthink exponents push their emotional arguments in the popular media and often put their names jointly, as an implied majority of scientists, on letters to politicians. They avoid scientific debate by ignoring any articles that sneak through challenging the conventional wisdom. Such rare articles are swamped by the sheer volume of contributions from groupthinkers.

In my case, the process was seemingly facilitated by *Wildlife Research* journal. After my *Ecological History* was submitted, thoroughly refereed and accepted as a *Review*, the journal's website announced its imminent publication. Before it was published, the Editors advised me they did not welcome my acknowledgement that they had motivated me to produce a review. They decided to rebadge it as a *Viewpoint*, implying a much lesser standard of scientific rigour, even though my 13 page article far exceeded the Journal's limit of four pages for viewpoints, otherwise called "*opinion papers*".

Here's the relevant correspondence:

> *Dear Vic*
>
> *I would like to clarify, as Editor, that as far as I am concerned, this is a Viewpoint article. This is what I communicated to Jenny.*
>
> *... I do not consider that it meets the criteria in terms of systematic and objective reviewing of the literature that would be required for a Review. ...*
>
> *Best wishes, Piran* [White, Professor of Environment, University of York, UK]
>
> *Thanks Piran,*
>
> *The fact is that I submitted it and you accepted it as a review. It's all there on Scholarone* [The Journal's online submission and review site]. *It was on this basis that I responded to your*

comments and criticisms. ...

Obviously I'm powerless to challenge you. Obviously, I no longer wish to acknowledge you or Andrea [Taylor, Monash University, Co-Editor].

Please just publish the paper!

Sincerely, Vic

Hi everyone,

We will remove the relevant lines in the Acknowledgements and retag the paper as a Viewpoint ...

Kind regards, Jenny [Foster[i], Publisher Wildlife Research]

On the same day as they published my *Review*, the journal published a response to a comment of mine[6] on an article which had incorrectly stated that koalas are extinct at Eden.[7] This *Rebuttal*[8] failed to meet any of the criteria normally required by the journal. Comments and responses are supposed to be published together, and if the authors of the original article fail to respond in a reasonable time, comments are meant to be published without a response. The *Rebuttal* was submitted four months after my comment and published nearly 12 months later. Comments are limited to 3000 words, and responses, supposedly to one page and 1000 words. Both comments and responses are supposed to be concise and impersonal.

The original article that I commented on was titled *Extinction in Eden ...* The *Rebuttal* stated that *"The argument over purported extinctions is a distraction"*. It was five pages long with 4700 words and was highly personal. It included the following terms: *missed the point, dismisses, no understanding, rejects, disputes, not reliable, Jurskis' belief, selective and contradictory anecdotes, distractions, no solutions, conjecture, cherry-picking, misused, baseless, logical error, assertion, ignored, conceptual*

---

[i] Dr. Foster's staff profile on CSIRO's website contains the following biography: *Experienced journals Publisher with a Ph.D. in Chemistry from the University of Melbourne. Deep knowledge of publishing ethics, permissions and copyright, editorial board management and strategic development. Strong communication and management skills.*

gap, inadequate, biased, exaggeration, flawed, polemic. I'm surprised that the editors didn't identify these failings when they reviewed my comment.

In the two years since my *Review* was published there has been no comment or reference to it in the scientific literature. Compare that to nine citations over a similar period of my less controversial paper about forest health in *Forest Ecology and Management.*[9] This *Review* also referred to irruptions of koalas in declining forests, and has now been cited at least 171 times in the international scientific literature, but never in relation to koalas.

San Diego Zoo has the biggest population of koalas outside Australia, with 20 on site and 30 on loan elsewhere. They had a *Fact Sheet* which stated: "**Beginning of European settlement:** *An estimated 10 million koalas existed around 1800 in Australia*". I advised them the *Fact Sheet* was incorrect and gave them a copy of my peer-reviewed *Ecological history of the koala.* They changed the text to "**Early European settlement** ..." and took advice from *experts* that there is *debate* about the abundance of koalas when whitefellas arrived. They said it would be helpful if I were able to "*cite peer-reviewed sources*".

After I sent them another *peer-reviewed source*, they removed any reference to the first century of European history in Australia:

> *Estimated that 10 million koalas existed in Australia when koala fur trade began in the late 1800s (Australia Koala Foundation, personal communication, 2018; also see AKF publication)*[10]

Their *Fact Sheet* still stated incorrectly that "*80% of koala habitat has been destroyed due to development, drought, and fires*". The *AKF publication* cited in the *Fact Sheet* stated that "*very little is known about the history and distribution of the Koala prior to the fur trade*". It seemingly dismissed Harry Parris' historical account of a koala irruption (Chapter 2), because Parris was a tram engineer rather than a "*learned scientist*". It also incorrectly stated that this was the only record of an irruption.[11] The Zoo's *Fact Sheet* does not refer to my *Review* with its abundance of historical and scientific evidence that their facts are incorrect.

My first book, *Firestick Ecology*[12], naturally discussed koalas. It received favorable reviews in the journals of the US based *Association for Fire Ecology*[13] and *International Association of Wildland Fire*[14]. There were no unfavorable reviews. Two years after publication, I asked the *Book Review Editor* for the *Ecological Society of Australia*, why they had not reviewed it. Dr. Perpetua Turner replied "*I contacted most of Australia's leading fire ecologists over a period of a year; all declined to review the book. I personally considered reviewing the book but could not write a balanced review*".

That's why scientific consensus is an oxymoron. Science cannot progress without debate. There is no scientific debate about koalas. There is currently a Senate Inquiry into *Australia's Faunal Extinction Crisis* and a Legislative Council Inquiry into *Koala Populations and Habitat in New South Wales*. I hope that this book will ignite debate.

Notes

1   Carrick 2017
2   Carrick 1990 Fig. 1
3   Gammage 2011
4   Arnold 2017
5   Jurskis 2017a
6   Jurskis 2017b
7   Lunney *et al.* 2014
8   Lunney *et al.* 2017a
9   Jurskis 2005
10   San Diego Zoo 2019
11   AKF undated
12   Jurskis 2015
13   McCaw 2016
14   Burrows 2016a

1

A POTTED HISTORY

Those who cannot remember the past are condemned to repeat it.... This is the condition of children and barbarians, in whom instinct has learned nothing from experience.

George Santayana *The Life of Reason* 1905

When whitefellas arrived in 1788, they didn't see any koalas in the open grassy valleys they sought to occupy. After a century, koalas were in plagues. Then their numbers crashed in Victoria, coastal New South Wales and south east Queensland, during the Federation Drought.[ii] In central and northern Queensland, they irrupted after the Federation Drought and declined during subsequent droughts. The historical crashes and declines in QLD were attributed to overly dense populations, drought, disease, predation by dingoes and foxes, and other factors.[1]

Modern experts blame hunting and/or clearing for all historical declines and crashes. Koalas were thought to be extinct in NSW by the 1930s.[2] However, a 1949 survey turned up 109 koala sightings across the State.[3] In 1966, Professor A.J. Marshall from Monash University wrote that *"few Australians have ever seen a wild koala"*.[4] Ten years later, *"the most significant outcome"* from a symposium at Taronga Zoo was *"unanimous agreement* [of 43 experts] *that the koala is no longer an endangered species"*.[5]

In 1976, there were *"large, growing populations"*[5] which

---

ii   A number of dry years between 1895 and 1903, extending to 1910 in coastal NSW and 1915 in southeast QLD.

irrupted into plagues once again. By 1999, NSW Roads and Traffic Authority was putting up warning signs.[6] Koala numbers in some areas inevitably crashed again during the Millennium Drought (1997-2009). A new generation of experts blamed clearing and climate change. AKF declared them *functionally extinct*.[7] WWF says they'll soon be gone, unless we donate money and change governments.[8]

All this time, koalas were breeding unnoticed in forests, just as they had for millennia. Unfortunately, the forests are once again starved of mild fire—trees are sick and scrub is booming —they are ticking time-bombs waiting to explode when ignited on hot windy days. Species that live off eucalypts are rampant. There are parasites, root rots, borers, sap suckers, and leaf eaters, including koalas. As trees die out, the irruptions can't be sustained and populations of arbivores eventually crash.[9]

Our genuinely endangered species need open, sunny, airy, grassy, healthy and safe bush. Just like people. Blackfellas didn't need boots, overalls, hard hats or fire engines to protect them from wildfires; they didn't plant trees, they burnt millions of baby trees and bushes every year. Whitefellas stopped Aboriginal management. Trees grew up, scrub choked out diversity and megafires exploded. As I edit my manuscript in spring 2019, there are hundreds of fires burning out of control in NSW and QLD. Many homes have been lost, people have been killed and there have been mass evacuations. No doubt, thousands of koalas have perished. History shows that this has nothing to do with climate.[10]

In 1992, the High Court rejected *Terra Nullius*.[iii] Eddie Mabo's legacy should have as much influence on land management as on land tenure. But green academics, bureaucrats and politicians don't get it. They claim to pay respect to Aboriginal elders past and present, then deny their monumental work across geological epochs. Our conservation policies are based on racism, specism, denial of history and junk science.

[iii] Land belonging to nobody—legally deemed as unoccupied.

Koalas are a rare species in healthy forests. Where they are plentiful, their numbers must inevitably crash, and fires will inevitably explode.

Notes

1   Gordon and Hrdina 2005
2   Lewis 1934
3   Anon. 1950
4   Marshall 1966
5   Bergin 1978 p. v
6   Museum of Applied Arts and Sciences 2018
7   AKF 2019
8   WWF 2019
9   Jurskis 2015 pp. 88-89
10 Jurskis 2015 pp. 162-163

2

THE SIMPLE TRUTH

Who is so deafe or so blinde, as is he,
That wilfully will neither heare nor see?

John Heywood 1546

Koalas are naturally rare because they eat tender, juicy and nutritious new leaves which are a rare commodity in healthy, mature eucalypt forests. Europeans set up camp at Warrane (Sydney Cove) in January 1788. When the first live koala was obtained fifteen years later, the Sydney Gazette reported[1] *"its food consists solely of gum leaves, in the choice of which it is excessively nice".*[iv]After another 130 years, the Director of the Australian Institute of Anatomy wrote *"The sole diet of the Koala consists of the tip leaves of certain types of gum tree".*[2]

They are solitary animals with large home ranges and they move long distances every night to find fresh new browse. Their big noses with an acute sense of smell allow them to sniff this out at a great distance. They have strong voices that carry a very long way on still nights so they can get together to breed. They breed prolifically, but most young cannot survive in healthy mature forest, because it is fully occupied by a small number of adults controlling very large home ranges. When an adult dies, a lucky young koala invariably finds the temporarily unoccupied

---

[iv]   Two centuries later, Dr. Bill Phillips claimed the newspaper report was *"wrong on both counts"*, apparently missing the key point about koalas' food selection. In 1933, childrens' writer Dorothy Wall had a better grasp of their basic ecology. She wrote that Blinky Bill's mother *"climbed down the tree, with Blinky following close behind, and went to another tree where they had a good meal of young leaves and tender shoots"*.

habitat, sets up home, thrives and breeds.

Most young male koalas travel long distances looking for food and somewhere to live. It's no real surprise that they've turned up in the dairy section of an Adelaide supermarket, on the bullbar of a fertilizer truck at Gunnedah or on oyster bags in Wapengo Lake—they're just following their noses and looking for a source of digestible protein that hasn't already been staked out by another koala. The real surprise is that expert ecologists can't grasp the basic concept of carrying capacity. Because koalas are cute and apparently cuddly, people assume that more is better.

Explorers and pioneers didn't see them because koalas didn't live in the open grassy woodlands of the river valleys that were sought by pastoralists. They are virtually invisible in forests because each large home range contains a single koala amongst thousands of trees. After Europeans cleared the valleys, established pastures and disrupted Aboriginal burning, koalas irrupted. Dense young forests grew up in the foothills, providing a feast of tender new shoots. Paddock trees in improved pastures got sick in the roots. They started to die back and reshoot. Continual resprouting of soft young leaves added to the feast. Expanding populations of koalas moved into the valleys.

In 1836, half a century after whitefellas arrived, Assistant Surveyor Govett was the first to observe an irruption of koalas.[3] He wrote that they *"are generally found in thick stringybark forests, and are numerous on the ranges leading to Cox's River, below the mountain precipices, and also in the ravines which open into the Hawkesbury River"* (i.e. the foothills of the Blue Mountains to the west of Sydney). Surveyor General Mitchell noted that these forests grew up because Aborigines were no longer burning, and that dense underwood choked out the grasses which kangaroos formerly grazed.[4] In 1840, Strzelecki found a similar situation in South Gippsland. His party avoided starvation by eating koalas because there were no kangaroos or emus to be had as they struggled for 26 days through 50 miles of dense young forest.[5,6]

Koalas in the Strzelecki Ranges epitomise the fecundity and resilience of the species. The 'Great Forest' was only 20 years old when the Polish nobleman and scientist battled through it in 1840. The Yowenjerre people had maintained an open grassy forest of big old trees with the firestick. After they were devastated by a smallpox epidemic in 1789[7], and virtually finished off by blood feuds with their neighbours[8], dense woody understorey spread from deep dark gullies and took over their country.[9] The dense scrub blew up when it was ignited by dry storms in extreme weather around 1820 and eucalypts germinated 'as thick as hairs on a cat's back'. Koalas were in plague proportions by the time Strzelecki arrived.

Much of the area was incinerated a second time in 1851, after Europeans settled in Victoria, when 5 million hectares exploded in the Black Thursday holocaust. There were two ages of young eucalypts, dating from the two megafires, when pioneers started clearing the Great Forest in the 1870s.[10,11] They found plagues of dingoes feeding on plagues of koalas. This was some of the most difficult, intense and extensive clearing of forest that has been done anywhere in Australia. Some koalas that were caught in the process were moved to islands in Westernport Bay, but high numbers persisted in the remaining forests.

At the same time, koalas were irrupting throughout southeastern Australia in the broad grassy valleys that were first occupied by pastoralists. By 1896, hundreds of thousands of koala skins were being exported from Australia, and a major Melbourne tannery was still sourcing its skins from South Gippsland.[12] The Red Tuesday fires burnt a quarter of a million hectares of the area in February 1898, and destroyed 2000 buildings. Twelve people died.[13] Undoubtedly, tens of thousands of koalas also perished. In December 1898, Victorian koalas were protected under the Game Act.

Clearing of the Strzelecki Ranges continued from west to east, and the region was mostly cleared by 1910.[14] Eight decades later, ecologists claimed that koalas had temporarily disappeared at the start of the 20th Century.[15] However, Fred Lewis knew differently.

In 1934, the Chief Inspector of Fisheries and Game wrote in *The Victorian Naturalist* that *"the species is almost extinct on the mainland, a very few Koalas surviving in ... South Gippsland ... I feel certain the Koala is doomed to early extinction"*.[16]

Lewis referred to the supposed *"extermination of the Koala in South Australia and New South Wales and ... its sadly depleted numbers in this State of Victoria"*. Modern ecologists attribute these crashes to the fur industry, but Victorian koalas were already protected from hunting. Fred Lewis was responsible for their protection. He blamed illegal shooting for *"sport"* and bushfires *"which, during the last twenty or thirty years have ravaged practically the whole of this State"*. Lewis' baseline was the 1880s, half a century after European arrival.

Some professional hunters apparently got around the Game Act by selling koala skins as wombat[14], and the Strzelecki koalas were undoubtedly devastated by the Red Tuesday fires, but the major factor in the crash of dense populations throughout eastern Australia was drought, especially the Federation Drought in the south[17]. Ironically, the hardy pioneers who cleared the Great Forest with their axes, actually blamed themselves for the drought.

Mr. T.J. Coverdale wrote: *"A study of the rainfall in relation to the clearing of the scrub is interesting, and shows a decline in the former, which if not owing to the clearing of the country, was certainly co-incident therewith"*.[18] In fact, the annual rainfall during the clearing phase was above, and immediately after clearing was below, the long term average of 1126 mm. The highest ever recorded was 1577 mm in 1952.[19] There are no records for the long period of Aboriginal management before the dense scrubby forest grew up, so there is no easy way[v] to assess any climatic impacts of its development or its subsequent removal.

---

[v]   Pollen, charcoal and sediment from cores covering the period during and after management by the Yowenjerre, might be compared with climate proxies to test this and disprove Mooney's and colleagues' flawed hypothesis that Aborigines didn't influence fire regimes. McKenzie's core from Powelltown, north of the Strzeleckis, covering more than 7000 years, may be relevant.[20]

Iredale and Whitley contributed to the same issue of *The Victorian Naturalist* as Fred Lewis in July 1934. They stated that "*we have been unable to trace any early reference to* [the koala's] *occurrence in this State. It must surely have been known by the middle of last century, yet no published information regarding Victorian specimens appears until the 'eighties. Perhaps our readers can supply some light on this problem*".[21] It was 1948 before the light was turned on by Harry Parris from the Goulburn Valley. He informed the Naturalists that there were no koalas in the valley when whitefellas arrived in 1839, but there were thousands by the end of the 1860s.[22]

The AKF takes great exception to this historical fact,[23] but Parris thoroughly reviewed the literature and oral histories. He established that koalas first appeared in 1856 and had irrupted into plagues by 1868. AKF wrongly challenges the history and rightly challenges Parris' opinion on cause: "*I believe this is because they were an easy meal for an aborigine*". Parris also stated that "*each traveller in Gippsland recorded bears*". Iredale and Whitley missed the historic reports from South Gippsland and thus did not understand its unique history.

This was the only place in Australia where explorers and pioneers saw koalas. When the *Chief Protector of Aborigines*, George Augustus Robinson, travelled along the south coast in 1844, four years after Strzelecki's expedition, his Aboriginal enforcers caught five koalas.[8,12] Ten years later, another whitefella and his black tracker saw a koala when it grunted as they hurried down a creek in pursuit of their quarry.[24] It was a genuine wilderness. Robinson wrote that "*the forest animals have vastly increased since the destruction of the local inhabitants*", arguing that koalas irrupted because the Yowenjerre people were no longer there to eat them.

Actually, the demise of the people and absence of their firesticks allowed the proliferation of a dense young forest that fed plagues of koalas and a scrub understorey which choked out the groundcovers, herbs and grasses that had fed kangaroos, wallabies and emus. When Europeans started clearing the scrubby forest in the 1870s they found stone axes and spearheads, grindstones and clay cooking ovens.[8,9,10,11,25] They recognised that it had been open grassy forest under Aboriginal management.

After they had toiled to clear the forest on the poorer soils of the steep country in the eastern Strzeleckis, many farmers walked off their land. By 1930, there were 60,000 hectares of abandoned farmland and another 65,000 hectares reverting to scrubby forest. Forests Commission Victoria started buying this land. In 1939 the Black Friday holocaust raged through the area. There were 14 other wildfires between 1899 and 1944. FCV commenced planting trees in 1949. Australian Paper Mills started buying abandoned farmland in the 1950s. In the 1960s, unproductive regrowth was cleared and plantings of pine and eucalypts were stepped up. More recently, Hancock Victoria Plantations took over the APM and FCV lands.[26,27]

HVP now manages 65,000 hectares of forest including 25,000 hectares of native forest reserves in the eastern Strzeleckis. Scientists from Monash and Southern Queensland Universities documented land use changes in this country since 1939, using a series of old aerial photographs. There was both clearing and regrowth in the first two decades after Black Friday, but the native forest area changed little over 60 years. The cleared land and unproductive regrowth has been put under plantations and bush has grown up on some roadsides and easements.[26] In 2009, the Black Saturday fires incinerated another 20,000 hectares of this area.[14]

Densities of koalas are still unnaturally high. In forests with monkey gum[vi], blue gum and/or yellow stringybark trees, they occupy home ranges of just over 3 hectares[14] (a density of 0.3 koalas per hectare). When Richard Appleton of HVP showed me around less than eight years after Black Saturday, it took me only a couple of minutes to spot one perched in a sick tree within an avenue of planted blue gums. Koalas are scarce in other types of bush, but these more natural, low-density populations haven't

---

[vi] *Eucalyptus cypellocarpa:* a species which koalas or 'monkey bears' were known to target for food.

been studied because they're hard to find, and ecologists don't seem interested in the bigger picture.

Recently, five scientists from various Victorian and Queensland Universities produced what they described as an *ecological history* of the koala in South Gippsland.[14] However, they somehow missed the importance of the Yowenjerre people and the dramatic changes in the landscape consequent to their demise. These scientists claimed that clearing and hunting after European occupation caused extreme declines and loss of genetic diversity in Victorian koalas. The South Gippsland population is supposed to be *"of high conservation significance as it has greater genetic diversity compared to other Victorian populations"*.

In fact, declines of koalas across eastern Australia followed their irruptions into agricultural lands **after** clearing. For example, the Cumberland Plain at Sydney was cleared by 1860[28] and koalas irrupted around its fringes from 1836 until the Federation Drought in the early 20th Century.[17] Koalas irrupted progressively a few decades behind pastoral development as it extended through the koala's range.[15,17,22,29,30] The least pronounced fluctuation was in north QLD, where development was late and not intensive. Koalas were first recorded there as uncommon in 1919.[30]

Massive clearing and repeated megafires had no impact on the viability of koalas in South Gippsland, which retained their full complement of genetic diversity. 'Reintroduced' populations in other parts of Victoria are said to lack genetic diversity after supposedly being squeezed through 'genetic bottlenecks'. However, there is no difference in genetic diversity between the native bred Strzelecki koalas and the supposedly reintroduced Cape Otway koalas. Their heterozygosity[vii] is within the range of northern populations.[31]

Koalas are not, and have never been, threatened with extinction as a result of European occupation and post-European development.

[vii] possession of different forms of genes at single locations on chromosomes

Notes

1   Anon. 1803
2   MacKenzie 1934
3   Anon. 1836
4   Mitchell 1848
5   Strzelecki 1845
6   Elms 1920 pp. 25-27
7   Flood 2006 p. 127
8   Wesson 2000 pp. 18-19
9   Holmes 1920 p. 73
10 Howitt 1891 p. 111
11 Coverdale 1920 pp. 45
12 Phillips 1990
13 Adams and Attiwill 2011
14 Wedrowicz *et al.* 2017
15 Lee and Martin 1988
16 Lewis 1934
17 Jurskis 2017a
18 Coverdale 1920 p. 33
19 Bureau of Meteorology 2019
20 Mooney *et al.* 2011 Table 1
21 Iredale and Whitley 1934
22 Parris 1948
23 Tabart 2019
24 Gammage 2011 p. 128
25 Dodd 1920 p. 148
26 Zhang *et al.* 2008
27 Wikipedia 2019 Strzelecki Ranges
28 AUSLIG 1990 p. 54
29 Lunney and Leary 1988
30 Gordon and Hrdina 2005
31 Kjeldsen *et al.* 2016 Table 1

3

GREEN PROPAGANDA

You can fool some of the people all of the time, and those are the ones you have to concentrate on.

George W. Bush, NFL dinner speech 2001

In Paris, on the 6th of May 2019, a *United Nations* committee announced that *"Nature is declining globally at rates unprecedented in human history – and the rate of species extinctions is accelerating"*. (Coincidentally this was May Day in Queensland.) The *UN* report didn't mention koalas, but *ABC News* in Sydney quickly rectified this deficiency. Next day, Lexi Metherell quoted Professor Watson, Director of Queensland University's *Centre for Biodiversity and Conservation Science*. He said *"we are world leaders in habitat clearance ... Thirty, forty years ago koalas were a common species"*.

A week later, *The Guardian* chimed in with a *Picture Essay* which included the seemingly posed photo of a koala with her joey perched on a windrow, which was used by *The Australian* a year and a half earlier to depict alleged destruction of koala habitat by logging (Introduction). The caption informed us that habitat loss is a major threat because clearing is progressing at a *"staggering rate"*.

This fake news is not new. Half a century ago, Professor Jock Marshall explained our mammal extinctions in the following terms[1]: *"It was the emergent skin hunters and timber traders who would be the first to do real damage. ... Soon, however was to come the Great Extermination. For this, the sheep farmer is almost entirely responsible ... In order to get more sheep to the acre ... Dad and Dave (and often Mum and Mabel too) set about ring-barking every tree on 'the place'".*

Marshall was the foundation Professor of Zoology at *Monash University*, but he got the story completely wrong. The trade in koala fur developed after koalas irrupted into plagues. Two centuries of timber getting hasn't extinguished, or even endangered, a single species of plant or animal in this country. Thirty years ago, Dr. Bill Phillips of *Australian National Parks and Wildlife Service* seemingly embellished the weird story of clearing in his book about koalas. He told us that we'd removed nearly two thirds of our tree-cover, causing the extinction of 18 mammals: *"the relentless clearing of forests cannot continue as it has for the past 200 years"*.[2]

In fact, 24 mammals became extinct during the 19th century in far western New South Wales where there was virtually no forest and no clearing. These were small and medium sized animals that relied on a diversity of groundcovers, herbs and grasses for their existence. When European pastoralists disrupted Aboriginal burning, dense growth of tussocks, shrubs and trees choked out their food plants.[3] We still had 88% of the treecover that had greeted whitefellas' arrival when Phillips wrote his book.[4] Three decades later, in 2018, Australia's State of the Forests Report showed that our forest area had increased by four million hectares during the previous five year reporting period.[5]

Now, Professor David Lindenmayer AO of *Australian National University* claims that timber harvesting causes megafires and threatens old-growth mountain ash trees as well as Leadbeater's possum. Actually, megafires unleashed by attempted fire exclusion have killed nearly all the old-growth mountain ash trees and countless possums, just as they have the old snow gums in Kosciuszko National Park where there is no timber harvesting.[3]

Against all the historical evidence, Lindenmayer and his

colleagues in the *Fenner School* continue to advocate fire exclusion. If they have ongoing success, the next alpine megafire will probably extinguish the mountain pygmy possum and the corroboree frog. These species are naturally rare because they live in restricted habitats—alpine boulder fields and bogs. They weren't endangered in the past, because these habitats were protected from wildfires by mild burning across the landscape—originally by Aborigines who visited the Alps in summer to feast on bogong moths, and later by seasonal alpine graziers. Since green academics and bureaucrats have succeeded in 'protecting' these habitats from grazing and burning, they have been incinerated by a succession of megafires.[3] After the 2003 alpine megafires, a former CSIRO scientist estimated that 370 million birds, mammals and reptiles were killed.[6]

Antisocial green propaganda, based on the wilderness myth, attributes all our imagined environmental woes to human activity. But people have been in Australia for at least 65,000 years.[7] Before European occupation, Aborigines maintained ecosystems and biodiversity across the country with mild fire for at least 40,000 years. When whitefellas disrupted Aboriginal management, species such as koalas that live in dense bush prospered. Species that rely on open sunny, airy, grassy bush declined. These are the truly endangered species, and the major threat to their survival is lack of ongoing human management.

Our rarest and most endangered snake is a good example. The broad-headed snake became extinct in Ku-Rin-Gai Chase National Park where there hasn't been any clearing or development, because we 'protected' the bush from mild fire and turned it into homogenous scrub. The snake is now disappearing from Moreton National Park where scrub is shading out its basking areas.[8] But scaly, cold-blooded creatures don't generate bankable emotional reactions. So they're not much use to multinational, taxpayer subsidised 'charities' such as WWF.

Koalas are only one of a wide range of native species that irrupt when we exclude sustaining fire and/or sow pastures, and our trees get sick. These include root pathogens such as Armillaria and Phytophthora[viii], root parasites such as native cherries; various borers that attack sapwood (e.g. longhorned beetles blamed for Tuart decline in Western Australia); leaf eaters, including weevils (blamed for Monaro Dieback) and Christmas beetles (blamed for New England Dieback); and parasitic mistletoes and vines such as devil's twine. Sap-sucking psyllids irrupt and sometimes attract plagues of bellbirds. Invasive understoreys such as wattles, casuarinas, ti trees and pittosporum respond to increasing light and moisture as the trees decline. Three-dimensionally continuous fuels build up and forests become ticking time-bombs ready to explode in dry storms.[10]

Grazing of native pastures by domestic stock can sometimes perform an ecologically analogous function to mild burning, by suppressing growth of woody seedlings and maintaining nutrient cycles that favour established trees, herbs and grasses. Exclusion of grazing from new reserves or rural residential developments has exacerbated problems created by suppression of mild fire across the landscape.[11]

Most ecologists and pathologists have got it exactly back to front. They think that koalas and fungi and weevils and beetles and understoreys are killing the trees. Exotic weeds such as lantana are favourite culprits. A new 'ism' has emerged in the scientific community. Pittosporum is allowed to run rampant because it's native[ix], whilst lantana is persecuted because it's exotic. Outbreaks of koalas in NSW and QLD are welcomed because they're cute animals. However, native weevils and longhorned beetles and Christmas beetles are a scourge to be dealt with. Plagues of mistletoes are lauded for attracting native birds, but plagues of psyllids that attract an aggressive native bird are shunned. Bellbirds are blamed for causing the psyllid

---

viii   Despite what most pathologists would have us believe, Phytophthora is native to Australia, originating in Gondwana.[9]

ix   Some Councils on Sydney Harbour remove pittosporum from their reserves. I recently provided evidence to NSW Land and Environment Court that a resident of Pambula Beach (South Coast NSW) had improved the environment by removing pittosporum from a neighbouring Council Reserve. He was convicted and fined for illegal clearing.

plagues of which they take advantage. Specism is as bad for our environmental management as is racism for society, because it replaces holism.

It is not politically correct to recognise koalas as an irruptive species—in plain English a pest.[x] So, green academics, bureaucrats, ENGOs and politicians have revised our ecological history. Plagues of koalas are portrayed as the norm, and the inevitable population crashes as crises. The original crashes were blamed on nasty, greedy hunters and pastoralists; the recent crashes on nasty, greedy pastoralists and miners and foresters and developers, and, of course, climate change. Stable, low-density populations have been misrepresented as critically endangered or extinct.

Green propaganda has been hugely effective. A Senate Inquiry— *The koala – saving our national icon*—reported: "*It is estimated that the koala population prior to European settlement was in the order of up to 10 million koalas*".[12] The Senate Report cited an AKF submission that referred to eight million koala skins exported between 1888 and 1927, more than a century after Europeans arrived.

The report also referred to Bill Phillips' book about koalas. Phillips made no reference to numbers prior to 1887 except the following: "*Although possibly restricted to the 'luxuriant brushes', as John Gould reported in 1863, there seems little doubt that koalas were present in large numbers*". Gould actually wrote that (in 1844) koalas were "*nowhere very abundant*" and could "*rarely be detected*". Consequently, he predicted their extinction. Phillips unaccountably described possum snaring and poisoning as koala hunting.[13] I've no idea why the Senate Committee bothered referring to Phillips' book. But I must admit that it was somewhat informative compared to another tome that was published 25 years later, titled *Killing the Koala*

---

[x] Former Federal Minister for Tourism, John Brown, achieved notoriety in the mid-1980s for, amongst other things, allegedly describing koalas as "*flea-ridden, piddling, stinking, scratching, rotten little things*" after he had 'cuddled' one in a 'photo opportunity'.

and Poisoning the Prairie.[14]

This was a 235 page political statement by C.J.A. Bradshaw, then Sir Hubert Wilkins Chair of Climate Change at Adelaide University, and US Population Control Guru Paul Ehrlich. The only mention of koalas seems to be a caption under a photo of a koala in Bradshaw's suburban garden:

> *Threatened in most parts of their range, koala populations are declining due to habitat loss, dog attacks, disease and inbreeding.*

I guess Bradshaw thought he was providing a good example in not having a dog and not clearing his garden. But I can't see why koala plagues are promoted as a good thing whilst people are told that they shouldn't have children.

In 2019, a Senate Inquiry into *Australia's Faunal Extinction Crisis* lapsed when Parliament was prorogued in preparation for a general election. On 3rd April, the Senate Committee for Environment and Communications released an interim report regurgitating propaganda about koalas. It stated that *"One significant example of the decline of a previously abundant species is the koala"*.[15] Leader of the Opposition and the Australian Labor Party, Bill Shorten, was almost universally tipped to win the election. One of his promises was to overhaul environmental legislation and establish a new Environmental Protection Authority. Shadow Environment Minister Tony Burke said that the changes *"will give us fair environment laws that make sure we are no longer the extinction capital of the world"*.

WWF with six other conservation or animal welfare NGOs produced a *Koala Habitat Conservation Plan.*[16] They announced that:

> *Just 230 years ago, many millions of koalas roamed the great forests and bushland of eastern Australia. ... The main driver of the loss and fragmentation of koala habitat are the weak and permissive laws passed by state, federal and local governments which allow excessive tree-clearing and deforestation. ...*
>
> *... Native forest logging on public lands needs to end immediately with the transferral of significant areas of state*

forest to the reserve estate. Expansion of the protected areas network is necessary to prevent further decline of koala populations. ... WWF has identified Koala Habitat Priority Areas ... More than 400,000 hectares of state forests, Crown land and other government lands ... Approximately 500,000 hectares of freehold land ... In Queensland, expansion of the protected areas network ... is required across all areas of the state where koalas occur.

The *ducks were all lined up*, but Shorten and the ALP lost the unloseable election.

A year earlier, New South Wales' Liberal-National Coalition Government had announced a similar strategy to supposedly stabilise and then increase koala populations by locking up more land. The main impediment to sensible land management for koalas or any other species is the lack of any brand differentiation between ALP and North Shore Liberals[xi] due to the success of green propaganda. Former NSW coalition Environment Minister Gabrielle Upton and her replacement Matt Kean, both fit the same bill with Tony Burke.

In any case, greens won't be satisfied until our environment, economy and society are destroyed, and all is wilderness, death and destruction. On 24th June, New South Wales announced that:

An Upper House inquiry has been established to inquire into and report on koala populations and habitat in New South Wales. Chair of the committee, Ms Cate Faehrmann MLC [The Greens], *said: "The committee recognises that there are grave concerns for the welfare of koalas in New South Wales. ... The inquiry will look into the current status of koala populations and their habitat and will focus on the impacts and effectiveness of existing policies relating to land management reform, forestry and the environment."*

In July, the Senate *"re-adopted"* the Inquiry into Australia's Faunal Extinction Crisis, for report by the last sitting of Autumn 2020.

[xi]   Liberal Prime Minister Tony Abbott was deposed by Malcolm Turnbull, before losing his seat to a seemingly green, left-leaning independent as a result of the political power of electorates north of Sydney Harbour with particularly 'well-heeled' demographics.

In August 2019, *NRMA Insurance* jumped on the koala bandwagon with a television advertisement:[17]

> *NRMA Insurance has begun a campaign to raise awareness of the plight of Australia's iconic koalas, by pledging to plant a tree every time it sells a home insurance policy.*

> *The IAG-owned insurer, which warns habitat destruction could wipe out the marsupials by 2050, has also launched a touching new advertising campaign featuring a boy rescuing a koala. ...*

> *"Every home is worth protecting," the company says. "We're helping koalas because koala habitat is under threat from deforestation, bushfires and climate change".*

Green propaganda has been hugely successful in raising funds and influencing governments and corporations, but of absolutely no benefit to conserving koalas or protecting them from bushfires. Meanwhile, megafires consequent to the successful propaganda contribute hugely to deaths and injuries of wildlife and emissions of greenhouse gasses.

Notes

1   Marshall 1966
2   Phillips 1990 pp. 96-97
3   Jurskis 2015
4   AUSLIG 1990 p. 55
5   Anon. 2018 p. 46
6   Hopkins 2019
7   Clarkson *et al.* 2017
8   Pringle *et al.* 2009
9   Arentz 2017
10 Jurskis and Underwood 2013
11 Jurskis 2005
12 The Senate. Environment and Communication References Committee 2011
13 Phillips 1990 p. 21
14 Bradshaw and Ehrlich 2015
15 The Senate. Environment and Communication References Committee 2019
16 WWF 2019
17 Insurance News 2019

4

JUNK SCIENCE

A quantitative, scientific method for deriving estimates of koala populations and trends was possible, in the absence of empirical[xii] data on abundances.

Fifteen Koala Experts, an Elicitation[xiii] Specialist and his Assistant, published in a Scientific Journal, 2016[1]

Koalas at Eden

In 1986/7, NSW National Parks and Wildlife Service (NPWS) organised a mail-out survey of koalas. They compared the returns of sightings since 1985 against all records of koalas before 1985 from this and previous mail-out surveys in 1949 and 1975. These records went at least as far back as the 1920s.[2] NPWS reported that koalas now mainly lived on the north coast, and had disappeared from hundreds of localities all across the State. They were supposed to live in rural areas, on good soils where valleys had been cleared for agriculture, rather than in forests.[3] This led to NSW listing the koala as a vulnerable species in 1992, when it was actually irrupting throughout its range[4] (Chapter 1).

Obviously, the dataset was extremely unbalanced in time and space. Nevertheless, a quick glance at the maps suggests that more sightings were reported from more places in 1987 than in 1975, and more in 1975 than in 1949. I suggest that a scientific analysis would have concluded that mail-out surveys cannot identify the distribution of a cryptic forest-dwelling species, and

---

[xii] Based on observation rather than theory
[xiii] Drawing out or bringing forth

that more koalas are seen when and where there are more people looking.

Tantawangalo State Forest in the Eden region was one of the great number of localities across the State where koalas were reported to have become extinct. Tantawangalo Catchment Protection Association (TCPA) was then lobbying to protect domestic water supplies against predicted impacts of timber harvesting. However, some harvesting trials were conducted in gauged sub-catchments without adverse effects.

In November 1990, TCPA located koalas within areas scheduled for harvest at Tantawangalo. There were persistent rumours that some 'spare' koalas had been flown in from the north coast. I believe that these rumours may have undermined the credibility to the local community of our data from subsequent radio-tracking studies of koalas across the region. By 1992, a total 470 person-days of field survey by TCPA and Forestry Commission had located 10 koalas. NPWS noted how hard it was to find koalas in the forest, and decided to do another mail-out to determine their distribution across the region! This was done a year later and published in 1997.[5]

Tantawangalo was now reported to be a core area for koalas, but private lands and National Parks supposedly weren't important.[5] The supposed key area of Tantawangalo was transferred to National Park in 1997.[6] In 2001, NPWS employed Mr Chris Allen, former member of TCPA and later President of South East Forests Conservation Council, a *"long-term campaigner against woodchipping"*,[xiv] to coordinate koala surveys. I had attended the media event where TCPA originally showed off their koalas in 1990. At that time, I was in charge of Forestry Commission Research at Eden. When asked by a reporter what I thought about it, I said something along the lines of: *I reckon it's great. Now that we've found koalas we can track them and find out how they operate in the forest.*

[xiv]   National Parks Journal April 2000 Vol 44 No 2 *Surveying Koalas*. National Parks Association NSW Inc.

Mr. Roland Breckwoldt of TCPA responded rather vigorously, seeming to imply that I was trying to claim credit on behalf of Forestry for finding koalas. Twelve months later, in November 1991, our Forestry Research Team radio-collared a koala at Tantawangalo and we started learning about the ecology of natural, low density populations. In November 1992, we caught a big buck in a very big yellow stringybark tree. It was a difficult capture and my slow reactions contributed to the animal's distress. However, we took it to a vet for examination and released it at the capture site with no permanent harm.

This koala was living in a mosaic of logged and unlogged coupes. It was spending a disproportionate amount of time in coupes that were regenerating from 'woodchipping'[xv].[7] After we tracked it for several months, in April 1993, *Sydney Morning Herald* published an article headed: ***Report attacks koala research.***[8] It began as follows:

> *The NSW Forestry Commission's koala research program in the south-eastern forests should be taken over by experienced biologists, according to two internal Government reports.*
>
> *The reports claim the commission's research will not properly assess the impact of logging on the small population of koalas in the forests west of Eden, one of the few natural populations remaining in NSW.*
>
> *In one of the leaked reports, a copy of which has been obtained by the* Herald, *the National Parks and Wildlife Service calls for a moratorium on logging and road-building operations in the forests and for an expanded research program into the koala population.*

Further on, the article stated:

> *The parks service report outlines Mr* [Roger] *Martin's findings that logging posed a grave threat to the koala population in the south-east, which he said might be a distinct genetic race important to the long-term conservation of the species.*

[xv] A seemingly derogatory term used by NPWS/OEH[2] for integrated harvesting of sawlogs together with poorly formed logs used to produce high quality paper for durable publications. Trees are retained for habitat and to supply seed to regenerate the forest.

Conservationists have joined the attack on the commission's research program after learning of a bungled attempt to trap one of the koalas. ...

A spokesman for the South-East Forest Alliance, Mr. Jeff Angel, said yesterday that the Government had been repeatedly warned of the "folly of allowing unqualified staff to undertake this work".

Obviously, our major disqualification was that we went into it with open minds, free of the apparently obligatory assumption that human activity is bad for the environment. The koalas certainly don't realise this. The first collar was a young male who came to investigate some road construction activity and grunted at a worker. Soon after, he travelled several kilometres to oversee harvesting operations from a tree at the edge of a log landing. He eventually covered more than 2000 hectares looking for somewhere to set up home before he was speared on the ground by a falling branch. Death by misadventure is the common fate of young males, as evident from the records at Port Macquarie Koala Hospital. Up there, they are usually killed by cars.[9]

An old male koala with worn-out teeth died of malnutrition and hypothermia when he became entangled in wire grass during unseasonably cold weather. He had not long before had the opportunity to pass on his genes when a mature female made a three kilometre round-trip into his territory. I wonder why the experts can't see that loud voices, good hearing, big noses, strong limbs and sustained fertility are perfect adaptations for solitary animals spread thinly across large areas of forest. Bellowing and fighting are very disruptive activities in unnaturally dense populations.

One of the favourite myths promoted by those, such as Mr. Allen of TCPA/NPWS, who would seemingly use koalas to prevent sustainable use of natural resources, is that they need big old trees.[10] What they really need is access to fresh young shoots when they're feeding, and somewhere safe and comfortable to sit when they're not. Most studies of koalas occur in areas lacking very large trees. None of the radio-collared koalas at Eden preferred large trees. The biggest koala preferred medium-sized trees over 50 centimetres diameter. The smaller males preferred trees over 30 centimetres. The youngest male used sapling/pole sized monkey gum under 30 centimetres in proportion to their availability.[7]

A juvenile koala used only saplings/poles. When you take nutrition, flavour and texture (species and leaf age preferences) out of the equation, it seems to be about arm span and tree diameter, i.e. the physics of climbing. A breeding female didn't use saplings/poles, even of the preferred species monkey gum, but there were plenty of these within her home range to sustain her growing daughter. Koalas sometimes roosted in dense shady trees that were not food species.[7] At Raymond Island, where koalas are supposedly overbrowsing their 'protected' habitat, I've observed koalas sunning themselves comfortably in convenient forks of dead trees with their backs to the wind on cold days (e.g. see Front Cover).

Altogether, we tracked eight koalas in three different parts of the region and were denied permission (by NPWS) to collar four more in three other localities. By 1997, these studies and a regional playback survey had established that there is a healthy breeding population through the region, which is infected by chlamydia, but without any expression of disease. Predators are common, but only two of 2000 samples of canid faeces collected from the forests in 1987 contained koala hair. The only other record of predation was a juvenile koala taken by a powerful owl—another rare species. Home ranges were between 38 and 580 hectares with an average of 169, corresponding to a density of 0.006 koalas per hectare. Eden koalas have slightly less genetic diversity than South Gippsland koalas, and slightly more than those on the Koala Coast.[7,11]

Two koalas lived in mosaics of logged and unlogged coupes, and preferred the regenerating forests. Another lived entirely in mature regrowth forest with no big old trees. Other surveys in the north-east of the region showed that koalas were using areas that had been recently 'woodchipped'.[7] However, the big difference I noticed between the ecology of the low-density population at Eden, and the high-density populations that are studied elsewhere, is that the high-density populations live in chronically declining forests.

NPWS shut down our radio-tracking studies and continued to rely on ineffective mail-out surveys to monitor the regional population. These surveys have repeatedly been used incorrectly to report local extinctions.[12] Mr. Allen was given oversight of extremely labour-intensive faecal pellet searches around State Forests in the northeast of the region. These searches produce very little ecological information at high cost[xvi], compared with radio-tracking surveys which produce a wealth of information, and playback or sound recording surveys which can effectively sample a whole region.

At the 2002 *Australian Koala Foundation* Conference in Ballarat VIC, I was presented with the *Golden Pellet Awards* bronze trophy. My paper was *Separating cause and effect: koala overbrowsing as a symptom of eucalypt dieback.*[13] However, the citation was "*for once, not saying that logging is good for koalas*". AKF still doesn't understand that there's no difference between Southern and Northern koalas. They can irrupt wherever there is an increase in soft young shoots.

Europeans occupied the Bega Valley in 1830 and saw no koalas until they irrupted in the 1860s. Despite heavy hunting for a lucrative skin industry, they increased to plague proportions by 1880. Dingoes increased markedly between 1880 and 1890. Numbers of koalas plummeted during the Federation Drought and they suffered epidemic disease from 1905 until they disappeared in 1909. Dingoes declined again as numbers of koalas crashed. Koalas persisted at very low densities in the surrounding forests.[12,14]

The regional population also persisted through the Millennium

---

[xvi] Pellet counts can identify some trees in which unidentified koalas may have roosted. They cannot identify home ranges. OEH have used them to estimate populations. In my opinion, these estimates are worthless.

Drought. A sub-population in dense regrowth from 1980s 'woodchipping' and wildfire in the north-east of the region, was irrupting by the 1990s. There were only 4 records of koalas in this area between 1920 and 1987. No koalas were found during intensive searches of 36 timber harvest coupes totalling 400 hectares in 1980.[3,15,16,17] No koalas were found by NPWS surveys in coastal forests between 1979 and 1984.[18]

Two koalas were detected from five sites during a regional playback survey in spring 1997—ten times the regional detection rate[11]. Faecal pellet surveys between 2007 and 2009 detected koala activity at an extraordinary 22% of sites in Mumbulla State Forest,[16] equivalent to detection rates by spotlight surveys of relatively high density populations in north coast regrowth forests.[19] By 2012-2014 koalas were detected at 24% of sites.[20]

In 2014, NSW Office of Environment and Heritage[xvii] apparently didn't consider at least 40 records of koalas in the south and west of the region[21,22,23] and incorrectly announced that koalas had disappeared by 1996, except in the north-eastern corner, where they had allegedly contracted into a *climate refuge*. They stated that the transfer of State Forest at Tantawangalo to National Park "*in 1999*" (which actually occurred on 1 January 1997[6]) had been "*too late for conserving the koala population*".[17]

Although OEH had reported finding koala faecal pellets at Tantawangalo in 2010,[16] they reported years later that none had been found.[17,20] They cited an unpublished, undated internal report to explain two different versions of results from the same faecal pellet surveys in 2010.[24] In 2014, Dr. Daniel Lunney and colleagues made a model supposedly showing "*regional loss of the koala over the past five decades*" (i.e. 1960-2010). In the same paper they said "*Our data showed shrinkage in the distribution of Eden's koalas... contracting progressively to the north-east of the region since European settlement*" (i.e. 1830-2010).[17]

[xvii] In respect of koala research, NPWS, DECCW and OEH are the same organisation with changing names.

In another paper, also published by *Wildlife Research*, they argued that a sighting of a koala in 2013 at Tantawangalo didn't prove that koalas were still there at that time.[24] (In November 2019, I saw a koala crossing the Princes Highway south of Eden, where they're also supposed to be extinct. I provided photos to the NSW Koala Inquiry on 9th December. Dr. Lunney was asked two questions relating to my evidence, but he wasn't asked about this koala that didn't realise it wasn't really there.)

Based on the alleged regional extinctions, OEH declared that plans to harvest timber in the northeast of the region needed to be *"revisited"*.[17] As a result, four Flora Reserves were established to 'protect' koalas, and timber resource was lost to industry in seeming contravention of the Regional Forest Agreement. A 2.5 million dollar subsidy was announced to obtain timber from further away.[25] That would cover a very large amount of carbon emissions!

In 2016, I visited the Mumbulla Reserve with two fellow conservationists. It took only three person hours to detect a female koala and joey in the declining regrowth forest (compared to 47 person days per koala in mature forest at Tantawangalo). After Kerry Rutherford spotted the koalas we found only two tiny faecal pellets (from the joey) on top of the deep litter amongst the dense shrubbery. The management plan for the Reserves will surely endanger koalas because it restricts mild burning. This is the same strategy that led to the loss of 60 homes at Tathra in March 2018, and some koalas may have been killed in the southernmost Reserve during this event.

Fig. 1 shows the historical trend in the koala population at Eden from European arrival to the present time (Lines 1d + 1a + 1d). Line 1a was published by NPWS in 1988[14] and shows that the population crashed after 1900 and then remained rare until the 1980s. Line 1d on the left shows the earlier history, that koalas were not seen after Europeans arrived until the 1860s. Line 1d on the right shows the later history: firstly, that koalas were increasing in the northeast and stable through the remainder of the region in 1997[5,7,11]; secondly, that koalas continued to increase in the northeast[12,20] and now, are also increasing in the south and west.

Lines 1b and 1c illustrate two alternative representations of the history by OEH. However, koalas were certainly not abundant in 1960 (Line 1b).[3,5,14,15] Nor were they in 1830 (Line 1c). The large area above Line 1c in the 19th Century and below Line 1c in the 20th Century, compared to Line 1a, illustrates the difference between the recorded history and the *"long-term trend ... of drastic decline"* reported by Lunney and colleagues from OEH.[17]

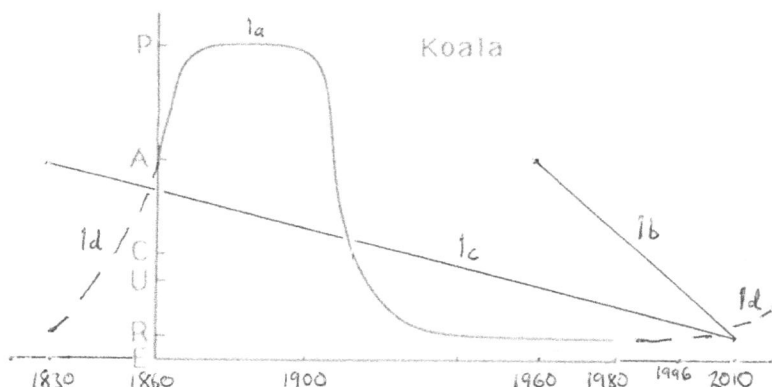

Figure 1: E extinct R rare U uncommon C common A abundant P plague
Title, Line 1a and y axis reproduced from *Australian Journal of Ecology*, by courtesy of *ESA*

Both Dr. Lunney[17] and Dr. Predavec[26] of OEH reported that koalas have been lost from the Eden region, except for the northeast corner. Dr. Bradley Law of NSW Department of Primary Industries (DPI) is co-editor of *Australian Zoologist* with these two scientists. Law has recently adopted a more efficient method of detecting koalas in forests by recording male bellows during spring. He and his colleagues employed the method during 2017 in the northeast corner of the region where koalas are known to be increasing, but not in the rest of the region where they are supposed to be extinct. A more conventional scientific approach would be to also use the method in the south and west to test the hypothesis that koalas are no longer there. Law's group found (male) koalas at an extraordinary 88% of sites (four times the detection rate of both sexes from faecal pellet surveys in the same area), but unaccountably reported it as a *low-density* [sub] *population*.[27]

Campbelltown

After European settlement extended across the Cumberland Plain near Sydney, koalas irrupted firstly in the west from 1836, and later in the south. At the turn of the century they were in plague proportions around Campbelltown (to the south) where they were hunted for their skins. Koalas occurred *"in almost every tree"*. However, OEH[28] wrote of an *"apparent population crash from the early part of the century and recovery in the 1980s"*. This second irruption began when suburban development extended into rural lands ~ 10 years after a major wildfire devastated the adjoining Sydney Water catchments in 1977.[8,29,30]

Alienation of formerly grazed and/or mildly burnt bushland for urban development and thick wildfire regrowth in the water catchments produced the second irruption of koalas that is represented by OEH as recovery. They incorrectly state that *"the population is low and always has been. ... historical clearing of fertile plateau land for agriculture and urban development resulted in an initial decrease in the Campbelltown population"*.[26] Remember that the fertile land was cleared by 1860 and koalas first irrupted after 1836 until ~ 1910.

A long-term radio-tracking study showed that the current *"low-density"* population is healthy and increasing, even though it was *"virtually unknown"* for the greater part of the 20th Century. Researchers suggested it is a *"dangerous idea"* that a low-density population of koalas (~ 0.03 per hectare[12]) might be viable, because the perceived vulnerability of this population has been used to supposedly 'protect' habitat for endangered non-iconic fauna, such as the broad-headed snake, *Hoplocephalus bungaroides*, in the same area.[30]

The density of this population is actually high compared to stable populations. This is evident because koalas are visible. The population is clearly irrupting, because young female koalas are establishing new home ranges adjacent to their mothers[30]. Carrying capacity of this habitat for koalas is temporarily increasing and decline is inevitable because the forests cannot sustain constant cycling of young foliage. Meanwhile, carrying capacity for other animals, such as the broad-headed snake, requiring open sunny conditions, is declining because of woody thickening.[31]

Coffs Harbour

Koalas were "*conspicuously absent from the explorer Clement Hodgkinson's account* [published in 1845] *of the tribes he encountered along the Bellinger River, in which he noted animals they consumed*". There were no records of hunting for skins, or historical photographs, and few oral histories of koalas at Coffs Harbour. A newspaper report from 1950 indicated that a resident in the area from 1896 to 1901 saw koalas, and there was a newspaper report of a koala crossing a road three quarters of a mile from Coffs Harbour in 1939. In an oral history recording from 1987, an 82 year old woman recalled seeing koalas in town around the late 1920s and early 1930s.[32]

A postal survey in 1990 attracted a respondent who saw a koala in Conglomerate State Forest as a young man in 1937, another who saw koalas at Nana Glen as a child around the 1950s and a third who saw koalas in dense scrub or "*up telegraph poles*" in Coffs Harbour in the 1940s. Apart from the foregoing, OEH found no records of koalas in the region prior to the 1960s.[32] Agricultural development around Coffs Harbour was limited by steeply dissected topography and thick forest. It was mostly confined to narrow creek and river flats.

Koalas apparently irrupted in the immediate vicinity of Coffs Harbour township around 1960 with the commencement of urban sprawl and consequent reduction of grazing and burning. OEH found many references to koalas from this time onwards and reported that koalas disappeared from some suburbs and localities as urban development progressed.[32]

At the same time, koalas were increasing in dense regrowth forests created by intensive harvesting using newly available post-war technology and equipment such as chainsaws and bulldozers. By 1991 koalas were strongly associated with these forests, being three times more frequent in heavily logged than unlogged forests.[19] By 2009, OEH[33] reported that this was one of only three areas in NSW where mail-out surveys showed that koalas were increasing.

Another mail-out survey in 2011 produced another increase in sightings at Coffs Harbour. OEH stated that *"While the raw data show an increase in the number of koalas … they do not account for the forgetfulness of people"*. So they *"downsampled"* postal survey data and *"adjusted"* it for *"forgetfulness"*. This turned a sampled increase in koala sightings between 1990 and 2011into *"a small, yet statistically significant, decline in the number of koalas of 4% over 21 years"*. They concluded that *"habitat loss has been relentless since European Settlement* and *the Koala population had been reduced from its pre-European size by 2000"*.[34]

North Coast

During the late 20th Century, koalas increased in dense young regrowth forests right across the north coast of NSW. For example, a survey of nearly 300 sites in 1991 found koalas at 22% of intensively harvested and regenerated sites compared to only 4%, on average, of unlogged or selectively logged sites.[19] After prescribed burning was reduced from the 1980s, chronic eucalypt decline extended through the forests and koalas began to irrupt. By the mid-1990s, koalas were detected at 46% of survey sites in the Upper Clarence and Richmond Valleys of NSW.[35] They became the most common arboreal mammal, occurring throughout forests where they had previously been uncommon[36]. By the turn of the millennium there were more than 20,000 hectares of severely declining forest in this area.[37] Now the area of declining forest has increased many times over.

Koalas and a range of other species including arbivorous insects, fungi and parasitic plants increased as forests declined. So-called Bell Miner Associated Dieback (BMAD) is a facet of this more general problem, which has attracted disproportionate attention. Bellbirds have irrupted in response to irruptions of psyllids in declining trees. Psyllids constitute plentiful, nutritious food for the birds in some types of declining forests.[12,37] Now there are not many coastal forests where you can travel any distance without hearing bellbirds. At the same time, there are many places where you can smell koalas as you walk along, as if you were walking past an enclosure in a wildlife park.

Between 2015 and 2017, aerial surveys by NSW DPI identified 44,000 hectares of BMAD, comprising about 4% of the survey area.[38] This is a huge underestimate of the area of declining forest, representing only areas of dead or near dead canopy. Forestry Corporation has identified that about a third of the forest area has impenetrable understorey.[39] Much more is thickly scrubbed but not yet impenetrable, and other areas of declining forest have thick litter layers or groundstoreys. The majority of the forest is declining in health.

During the same period, Dr. Bradley Law and colleagues from DPI "*sampled a broad range of timber harvest intensities and times since harvesting, at both site (~ 300 m radius) and a larger landscape scale (1 km buffer), together with old growth forests for comparison*" across the north coast. They found (male) koalas at 64% of sites irrespective of: whether there had been any logging; the intensity of logging; or time since logging. Koalas have increased throughout the declining forests since 1990, occurring at densities of more than 0.03 per hectare. They are no longer associated with young regrowth.[12,40] These DPI researchers apparently haven't noticed the widespread chronic decline in forest health. They haven't reported it or discussed the implications for koalas.

Law's team suggests that sound recordings are five times more effective than conventional field survey techniques. This seems to be an overstatement because they haven't accounted for the initial increases of koalas in dense regrowth or the subsequent increases in declining forests. Meanwhile, OEH's ineffective mail-out survey technique has morphed into *"internet-based participatory mapping survey"* otherwise known as *"geographic citizen science"*. But it's still no use for studying cryptic forest-dwelling animals. Nevertheless, it is used and promoted as state of the art science.[41]

For example, five universities, four regional councils, OEH and *Friends of the Koala*, collaborated in a north coast study:

> *This study examined the validity of crowdsourced wildlife (koala) observations from the two perspectives of validity-as-accuracy and validity-as-credibility. The validity-as-accuracy perspective analysed the accuracy of crowdsourced observations against a koala likelihood model using multiple measures of spatial concurrence while the validity-as-credibility perspective examined participant variables as potential sources of greater or lesser accuracy. There was significant spatial association between crowdsourced koala observations and the koala likelihood model. Where there were differences in the spatial results, there was lower confidence in the likelihood model due to fewer historical koala observations. Thus, there is the possibility that crowdsourced observations may represent more recent, changed conditions in the distribution or numbers of koalas within the study area. More accurate koala observations were contributed by older citizens with a higher level of self-rated knowledge of koalas, a higher level of formal education, and who had lived in the study area longer.*

> *There are several important implications from this study. The first is that crowdsourced wildlife observations, if sufficient in number and geographic scope, can be used to cross-validate and update wildlife distribution models. Wildlife populations, such as the koala, are dynamic, especially in a study area experiencing significant pressures on the populations from loss of koala habitat, human-induced mortality (e.g., from cars and dogs), and the spread of infectious diseases.[41]*

In plain English—a recent unbalanced, i.e. biased, set of casual observations of a cryptic species was tested against a model based on earlier biased casual observations, and found to be better because there were more observations. This was despite supposed pressures from clearing, cars, dogs and disease. The most important implication is that more observations can be used to update models that are, in any case, of no real use. I suggest that balanced sampling using an efficient survey technique that actually works in the bush would be a more scientific approach. In the meantime, accumulation of more sightings in a shorter time period suggests that koalas are increasing.

Obviously, that's not how the experts see things. They concluded as follows:

> – the north coast of NSW has almost every koala conservation and management problem that exists, except for crippling droughts as experienced in the drier regions west of the Great Divide and overpopulation. ... detailed, on-ground, labour-intensive surveys are not feasible except in a few locations. Geographic citizen science ... provides a way forward so that ... government ... can gain a reliable grasp of the conservation and management issues facing koalas ... citizen science spatial surveys are a useful investment ...[41]

However, a consultant's report to OEH, obtained under the *Government Information (Public Access) Act*, states that data obtained from such surveys are biased towards rural and regional centres, and State Forests where there have been field surveys, whilst they underestimate koalas' occurrence in existing National Parks.[42] So they can be very useful to anyone who might like to use public concern about koalas to support calls for an increase in National Parks at the expense of State Forests.

More Generally

Despite three separate rounds of deliberation by the Federal Government's Threatened Species Scientific Committee, a Senate Inquiry, 'workshops' involving our "*most experienced koala ecologists*", a partial listing under Commonwealth environmental legislation and the subsequent publication of a Review in *Biological Conservation*[43], Australians remain in the dark about the basic ecology of koalas. A large part of the reason is that journals tend to reject articles challenging material that they have previously published.

A week after my *Ecological history of the koala*[44] was released, *British Ecological Society*'s *Journal of Applied Ecology* published an article by ecologists who claimed credit for reversing a supposedly *"long-term"* decline over *"two decades"* in a sub-population of koalas in south-east QLD, by controlling wild dogs and chlamydiosis.[45] I submitted a comment pointing out that it was not a long-term decline and it was not caused by predation and disease. It was an inevitable crash following an irruption. It occurred during the Millennium Drought, just as a crash during the Federation Drought had followed the original irruption in the late 19th Century.

Here is an extract from my submission:

> Apart from the vague reference by Gould, koalas were not reported at Moreton Bay prior to 1900, when they suddenly became abundant (Gordon and Hrdina 2005, Fig 3). It is clear that they irrupted in the late 19th Century.
>
> Since then, their abundance has varied with rainfall. Koala numbers crashed early in the Federation Drought, recovered after above average rainfall in 1903 and 1906 and crashed again after drought returned in 1907. They recovered slightly after high rainfall in 1921 and average rainfall in 1924. Numbers were increasing again in 1930 after three years of high rainfall, despite a high take by hunters during the final open season in 1927 (Gordon and Hrdina 2005).

An Editor rejected my comment in the following terms:

> I find the manuscript does not have the quality, in writing or scientifically, to be sent to reviewers. The arguments presented are not well-articulated or well supported, and I found at least one instance in which Dr. Jurskis appears to have misrepresented the literature to support his views.
>
> In the manuscript and appeal Dr. Jurskis writes "koalas

were not reported at Moreton Bay prior to 1900, when they suddenly became abundant (Gordon and Hrdina 2005, Fig 3)." This is strange, because Gordon and Hrdina do not report a sudden increase in abundance in 1900 (indeed, their Fig. 3 does not hint at the trend before 1900).

(I've given up trying to alert Editors that I'm not a Dr. They seem to assume that someone without a PhD is incapable of making a scientific contribution.)

Gordon's and Hrdina's Figure 3 shows "*Records of koala numbers from 1890-1940*". There were no records of koalas in Moreton Bay District between 1890 and 1900. Dr. Greg Gordon informed the Journal as follows:

In my 2005 paper I did not comment on koala abundance prior to 1890 as my work was dealing with later periods associated with the koala fur harvest. However, I fully agree with Vic Jurskis that abundance in that region increased greatly in the late 19th century. His survey of the historical literature for koala reports clearly shows the paucity of reports in the early and mid 19th century and I believe he is correct in concluding that koalas were scarce during this period and that an irruption occurred sometime in the late 19th century.

I advised the Journal "*I am very deeply concerned that* [an Associate Editor] *has wrongly made a very serious allegation that I* [apparently] *misrepresented the literature and that this has been accepted by the Senior Editor*".

The journal responded:

Thank you again for your further correspondence on this matter. Clearly, there is a difference of interpretation over one of the cited papers. That point notwithstanding, however, it remains that both editors felt that the clarity and flow of your arguments were not up to the level required by this journal ...

Biological Conservation – the journal

In 2015, this journal which is affiliated with the US-based *Society for Conservation Biology*, published a *Review* of koala conservation.[43] It summarised the evidence assembled by "*17 of Australia's most experienced koala ecologists*". The paper had 18 authors so it wasn't clear which scientist didn't claim expert status. The title was: *Conserving koalas: A review of the contrasting regional trends, outlooks and policy challenges.* It reported that "*Population declines are common in the northern half of the koala's range, where habitat loss, hotter droughts, disease, dog attacks and vehicle collisions are the major threats. In contrast, some southern populations are locally overabundant and are now subject to managed declines.*"

In 2019, I submitted a *Perspective* article to the journal. Their *Guide for Authors* specifies that:

> *These articles provide an opportunity for authors to present a novel, distinctive viewpoint on any subject within the journal's scope. The article should be well grounded in evidence and adequately supported by citations but may focus on a stimulating and thought-provoking line of argument that represents a significant advance in thinking about conservation problems and solutions. Perspectives articles should not exceed 8000 words.*

Here is the start of my article:

Abstract

> *I argue that the listing of koala as a species partially vulnerable to extinction is unjustified. I place the recent crash of the Koala Coast population in a wider geographical, historical and ecological context. Koalas are resilient and often behave as a pest. They have repeatedly irrupted to unsustainable levels in dense forests and declining stands of eucalyptus. Dense populations inevitably crash during droughts. Both conservation and animal welfare can be easily addressed. The priority must be restoration of healthy ecosystems by frequent mild burning.*

Introduction

> *... At the Koala Coast, near Brisbane (QLD), the population was considered to be secure at the turn of the Millennium, but declined by three quarters during the ensuing decade, providing impetus for the Commonwealth listing. Clearing, climate change, disease, predation and road accident trauma were blamed for this and other declines in the north. In the southern States (SA, VIC), koalas continue to irrupt and actions are necessary to control their numbers (McAlpine et al.*

2015). The irruptions are supposedly consequences of limited genetic diversity in reintroduced populations (e.g. Amis 2014, Department of Environment 2019) or absence of diseases and predators (e.g. Menkhorst 2008).

However, the history of the Koala Coast, formerly the Moreton Bay District, is typical of the history across the species' range. Koalas irrupted after Europeans disrupted Aboriginal burning and established exotic pastures. Populations crashed early in the 20th Century and irrupted again before crashing at the turn of the Millennium. Holistic ecology points the way to restore ecosystem health, conserve koalas and protect their welfare.

Here is the response from the Editor:

Article transfer offer-The koala is a resilient species that can be easily conserved

Dear Dr. Jurskis,

Thank you for your submission to Biological Conservation. Having now evaluated your manuscript, I feel there are other Elsevier [the publisher's name] journals that may better suit the scope.

Please click on the link below to find out more about the alternative journals I recommend ...

Here is my reply:

Dear Professor Lian Pin Koh,

Thank you for the offer to transfer the article. I rely on a superannuation pension and have no other sources of funding. I cannot afford to pay AUD2400 plus tax to have an article published. I note that the suggested journal has less than half the impact factor of Biological Conservation. My submission is directly related to three articles published in Biological Conservation, including a Review ...

I found out that the *Article transfer offer* was effectively a rejection:

Thank you for your email. I have no doubt that you have invested significant effort into the preparation of your article. Our decision on your manuscript is in no way an indication of its quality.

A key consideration for publication in this journal is that the study must advance the science and practice of conservation biology, and thus have broader application for a wide international audience. We believe that your manuscript would be more suitable for a more specialised journal.

The current status of your manuscript is 'Rejected'. ...

So I objected to the Editor in Chief:

My submission relates directly to a Review published in your journal that was apparently judged to "advance the science and practice of conservation biology, and thus have broader application for a wide international audience" *My submission challenges the validity of that review. It must therefore have broad application for a wide international audience. I ask that you reconsider your decision.*

Here is his response:

Your paper clearly has values and is indeed well connected to existing papers. But, in the meanwhile, it is too descriptive and focused on a single species to make a contribution to the journal. This does not undermine your perspective. I am sure it will be relevant for koala conservation and probably for other species. But other targets ... are more appropriate.
All the best,
Vincent [Dr. Devictor, CNRS – French National Centre for Scientific Research]

I tried again:

Dear Vincent,

*You published a **Review** on the same single species, that is historically and ecologically flawed. That review stimulated international media coverage,* [in my opinion] *misrepresenting the situation of the species and ensuring ongoing waste of multimillion dollar expenditure, supposedly on conservation of the species, that could be diverted to funding real action on conservation of really threatened species. ...*

Why do you bother pretending to encourage different perspectives? I realise from bitter experience that you're no different to most editors in this respect, but ecological science and conservation cannot advance while ever journals [seemingly] *suppress debate.*
Sincerely,
Vic

The Editor in Chief responded:

Dear Vic,

I understand your frustration. But I am not sure I understand your accusation for "defending unscientific groupthink" or of "debate surpression" sic My feeling is that we are very open to debates. ... If you wanted to write a response letter to the review mentioned; this is fine. Authors will respond, and a correspondence, if respectful and constructive, will be published. ...

Best,

Vincent

So I accepted his offer:

Thanks Vincent,

I will certainly submit 2 responses to the articles that I cited. However there is so much wrong in the Review that I can hardly scratch the surface in 800 words and 5 citations. Then the authors who have already been allowed 12,000 words get an equal right of reply! ...

Best regards,

Vic

I submitted a letter:

Conserving koalas should be easy: Response to McAlpine et al.

McAlpine et al. (2015) reported a consensus in 2012 of "17 of Australia's most experienced koala ecologists" (hereafter experts) on recent (decadal) population trends, their causes, threats to koalas and complex challenges for conservation. This led to listing of the koala as vulnerable to extinction in two thirds of its range and recent calls in the media for it to be listed as endangered. The decadal trends missed the greater part of the koala's ecological history. Supposed causes were incorrectly assigned to regional trends that are not fundamentally "contrasting", but rather out of phase. Koalas were naturally rare and have repeatedly irrupted and declined at different times and places since Europeans occupied Australia (see Jurskis 2017).

Their natural habitat is forest dominated by mature eucalypts with poor, hard, dry leaves. So they occupy large home ranges and move long distances nightly to find fresh browse. Explorers and pioneering pastoralists did not see koalas in the open riparian woodlands they sought to develop. However, the experts now regard these as high quality habitats and "refugia". Naturalist, John Gould, was first to predict the koala's extinction when he found very few, despite help from Aborigines, in 1839/40.

Koalas irrupted progressively through their range, decades after Europeans disrupted Aboriginal burning and established exotic pastures. Dense growth of young eucalypts in foothills and chronic decline of established trees created a bounty of soft, juicy, nutritious young leaves. Populations crashed during the Federation Drought in the early 20th Century, when declining trees in valley pastures could no longer sustain continual resprouting of young leaves. High levels of disease and predation by dogs or foxes coincided with population crashes in some areas. The experts attributed the historical crashes to "hunting for fur". *They did not acknowledge the prior irruptions, nor that koalas had increased for decades whilst being hunted before the drought. Very low density populations persisted, mostly unnoticed, in forests.*

Late in the 20th Century, koalas increased in dense regrowth forests created by intensive logging or wildfires, and in new plantings for timber or amenity. At the same time, prescribed burning and grazing were reduced and chronic decline of eucalypt forests became increasingly widespread. Consequently, koalas irrupted widely. For example, koalas had been strongly associated with dense regrowth created by high-intensity logging in northern coastal NSW, but now they are common right through the forests, whether recently heavily logged, old growth or somewhere in-between (Law et al. 2018).

During the Millennium Drought, many dense koala populations inevitably crashed, whilst low-density populations remained stable or continued to increase. The experts attributed declines to habitat loss, climate change, disease, dog attacks and collisions with vehicles. A sharp decline on the Koala Coast did not coincide with habitat loss. This was explained as "extinction debt, where populations continue to decline long after the main habitat destruction occurred". *The experts alluded to major destruction of koala habitat before 1996, but presented no evidence of any decline in koalas prior to the onset of drought.*

In 2005, the largest continuous habitat with the largest koala population in the Murray-Darling Basin of NSW was reserved in The Pilliga. The population had irrupted from "exceptionally low numbers … throughout most of the last century", *however it crashed again during the Millenium Drought (Lunney et al.*

2017). Habitat loss was not a threat and extensive reservation of habitat did not protect it. The experts attributed the crash to climate change. Conversely, Lunney et al. (2017) found that koalas persisted at relatively hot and dry sites. They seemingly contradicted this by stating that "koalas are being lost evenly … including in the moist riparian habitats*".*

Some dense populations, supposedly in prime riparian habitats, were extirpated and others crashed during two extreme droughts on a centennial timescale. Low-density populations, occupying supposedly poor quality habitats in NSW and QLD, persisted unscathed through both events. The kinds of surveys that informed the experts' consensus and Lunney's et al. (2017) report, cannot determine presence/absence or dynamics of low-density populations (e.g. Law et al. 2018), and have repeatedly supported incorrect reports of local extinctions (McAlpine et al. 2015, Jurskis 2017).

For example, when koalas were translocated south from Sydney into supposedly unoccupied habitat, local koalas appeared and bred with the immigrants (Close et al. 2015). The experts consider that koala numbers are "critically low*" near Eden and stable or increasing near Sydney. In reality, a resilient low-density population extends 500 km through continuous habitat from Eden to Sydney, with some nodes where subpopulations are irrupting (Close et al. 2015, Jurskis 2017).*

Management for conservation of all biota should focus on reinstating mild fire to maintain healthy and diverse ecosystems with low densities of koalas in reserves and higher, but sustainable densities in multiple-use forests.

References

Close, R., Ward, S., Phelan, D., 2015. A dangerous idea: that Koala densities can be low without the populations being in danger. Australian Zoology 38, 1–8.

Jurskis, V., 2017. Ecological history of the koala and implications for management. Wildlife Research 44, 471-483.

Law, B.S., Brassil, T., Gonsalves, L., Roe, P., Truskinger, A., McConville, A., 2018. Passive acoustics and sound recognition provide new insights on status and resilience of an iconic endangered marsupial (koala Phascolarctos cinereus) to timber harvesting. PLoS ONE 13: e0205075.

Lunney, D., Predavec, M., Sonawane, I., Kavanagh, R., Barrott-Brown, G., Phillips, S., Callaghan, J., Mitchell, D., Parnaby,

H., Paull, D.C., Shannon, I., Ellis, M., Price, O., Milledge, D., 2017. The remaining koalas (Phascolarctos cinereus) of the Pilliga forests, north-west New South Wales: refugial persistence or a population on the road to extinction? Pacific Conservation Biology 23, 277-294.

McAlpine, C., Lunney, D., Melzer, A., Menkhorst, P., Phillips, S., Phalen, D., Ellis, W., Foley, W., Baxter, G., de Villiers, D., Kavanagh, R., Adams- Hosking, C., Todd, C., Whisson, D., Molsher, R., Walter, M., Lawler, I., Close, R., 2015. Conserving koalas: a review of the contrasting regional trends, outlooks and policy challenges. Biological Conservation 192, 226–236.

The Editor's decision was:

> I regret to inform you that reviewers have advised against publishing your manuscript, and we must therefore reject it. Please refer to the comments listed at the end of this letter for details of why I reached this decision ...
> Kind regards,
> Vincent Devictor
> Editor-in-Chief Biological Conservation
>
> **Comments from the editors and reviewers:**
> **-Reviewer 1**
> No comment.

At the bottom of the email was a link to a pdf file—*Clive McAlpine Response July 8*.

I replied to the Chief Editor:

> There are no reviewers' or editors' comments at the end of your 'letter'. There is only a response apparently from Clive McAlpine that doesn't meet the specifications you advised for correspondence. It is over 1400 words with 9 references and does not address the issues raised in my letter. It is disrespectful. There is no evidence that my letter and the response have been impartially assessed by your editorial team or any reviewer. Please review my letter, the response and my brief (1 page) comments (attached) so that you can make an informed decision on publication of this correspondence.

The final word from the Editor was:

> I took the decision based on my review of what I had in hand: your letter, their response and the general context. I went back

to the arguments, to the initial paper and I do not consider that this correspondence will be useful. ... The response from Clive McAlpine will not be published either.

Apparently, consensus rules. To give you an idea of what an open debate might look like, I've reproduced hereunder McAlpine's *et al.* response, with my comments, which the Editor declined to consider, interposed in italics:

A response by McAlpine *et al.* to the letter criticising their paper ...

Consider the title of the correspondent's letter to the editor: "Conserving koalas should be easy: Response to McAlpine *et al.*" We asked, what does the author see as the easy solution? We found the answer in the correspondent's final sentence: "Management for conservation of all biota should focus on reinstating mild fire to maintain healthy and diverse ecosystems with low densities of koalas in reserves and higher, but sustainable densities in multiple-use forests." The correspondent asserts that the optimum, indeed the only way, to manage koalas is by the logging of native forests, accompanied by prescribed burning regimes, and without any evidence or discussion, contends that this is the way to manage all our biota. This is, in our opinion, an unsustainable argument.

Paragraph 2: I made no such assertion. I recommended reinstatement of mild fire regimes. I pointed out that higher densities of koalas can be sustained in dense young forests. I did not discuss other biota because I was limited to 800 words. Other biota were discussed in my full length paper that you rejected because it was supposedly not within the scope of the journal.

Now consider the opening sentences of the correspondent's letter: "McAlpine et al. (2015) reported a consensus in 2012 of *"17 of Australia's most experienced koala ecologists"* (hereafter experts) on recent (decadal) population trends, their causes, threats to koalas and complex challenges for conservation. This led to listing under the Commonwealth Environment Protection and Biodiversity Conservation Act 1999 of the koala as vulnerable to extinction in two thirds of its range…"

There is a better interpretation of the reason for the listing. In 2011, the Senate undertook an enquiry into the koala and recommended that the Commonwealth government reconsider the koala, with a view to recognising it as a threatened species. As a result, the Commonwealth scientific committee considered the issue in detail and did list the koala in 2012 as vulnerable for NSW, Queensland and the ACT, but not for Victoria or South Australia. This is the more likely candidate for the listing than the paper by McAlpine *et al.* (2015), published three years *after* the listing by the Commonwealth.

*Paragraph 4: I did not suggest that the 2015 paper led to the listing, I suggested that the February 2012 **consensus** led to the listing in May 2012. All the experts informed the deliberations and 13 of the 17 are cited in the listing advice, many several times. I'm happy to substitute* supported *for* led to.

The McAlpine *et al.* 2015 paper addressed ways of stemming the losses, not one that promoted the case for listing as threatened. *sic* An important paper from the Australian Centre for Ecological Analysis and Synthesis (ACEAS) expert workshop held in July 2012 was the one dealing with estimates of numbers and the rates of decline of koalas (Adams-Hosking *et al.* 2016).[xviii] The fact that the correspondent missed it is a major oversight, and reveals that the correspondent was poorly acquainted with the key koala papers, and more intent on promoting logging and burning as the universal nostrum[xix] for all things conservation.

Paragraph 5: My letter pointed out that "the losses" are inevitable consequences of unnatural irruptions. I was limited to a maximum of 5 references. I did not promote logging.

Furthermore, an egregious misreading by the correspondent of one paper (Lunney *et al.* 2017) reveals an inability to correctly state what the authors found. The correspondent states that: "The experts attributed the crash to climate change." Lunney *et al.* (2017) found a five-fold decline in the koala populations of

---

[xviii] These were the 'quantitative, scientific estimates based on no empirical data'.
[xix] An ineffective medicine prepared by an unqualified person or charlatan

the Pilliga forests of northwest New South Wales from the early 1990s to 2014. There is no contradiction in the Pilliga paper, the contradiction only appears if you cherry pick the environmental variables (hot and dry). What the paper actually said was:

Paragraph 6: The experts stated that "Climate change is a major threat" *and* "The observed substantial decline *[in The Pilliga]* appears due to an extended drought (2001-2009) combined with extended periods of above-average temperatures".

"Persistence is a different way of looking at population change and one that is complementary to looking at declines. In the case of the Pilliga, koalas persisted at sites that showed certain environmental characteristics: the persistence sites were relatively hot and dry with conditions making them susceptible to fire; they had not been burnt according to available fire-history mapping; the soils were deep, had a high water-holding capacity and relatively high nitrogen availability; and they mostly were located close to drainage lines. This pattern was reinforced when investigated against the Mitchell Landscapes, with more persistence in floodplain and channel landscapes. These results reinforce the location of sightings of koalas during the repeat surveys next to drainage lines primarily in the western half of the forests and is consistent with that seen in other studies in semiarid landscapes."

Paragraph 7: Lunney et al. (2017) stated that "Sites where koalas persisted between the two survey periods can be characterised **primarily** by Factor 1: sites that were hot (Fig. 2h, i) and dry (Fig. 2j) relative to other sites in the Pilliga".

McAlpine *et al.* (2015) reported this decline but did not directly attribute it to climate change, although similar case studies were reported. For example, in southwest Queensland, Seabrook *et al.* (2011) demonstrated that climate change (the increased frequency of severe heatwaves combined with drought) is having a devastating impact on koala populations. It would appear that the correspondent seems to disregard the over-riding importance of climate change. We also note here that the term "experts" is used disrespectfully, and we can presume that disrespect was intended earlier in the piece.

Paragraph 8: Refer to my comment on Paragraph 6.
The citation of Seabrook and others is not relevant to my letter.
I was limited to 800 words. 'The experts' is 2 words, 'McAlpine et
al 2015' is 4. My letter is 799 words. They described themselves
as "Australia's most experienced koala ecologists". *I accepted*
this. There is no disrespect.
However, their response contains these disrespectful terms:
anecdotal, bias, cherry pick, disregard, disrespect, egregious,
fails, flawed, inability, incredibly naïve, major oversight,
misguided, neither sensible nor possible, nostrum, not worthy,
poorly acquainted, terrible, undermines, uninformed.

The lack of a national synthesis and interpretation of recent
regional koala population trends was the motivation for McAlpine
et al. (2015). It was based on an earlier ACEAS workshop held
in February 2012, with 18 of the leading koala researchers
representing all states with koala populations participating. (We
point out that our paper has 18 authors, not 17, as mis-stated by
the correspondent.)[xx] The synthesis drew on available published
literature and the knowledge of the participants. It concluded
that population declines are common in the northern half of the
koala's range, where habitat loss, hotter and more severe droughts,
mining infrastructure development, disease, dog attacks and
vehicle collisions are the major threats. In contrast, some southern
populations are locally overabundant. The koala presents the
problem of managing a wide ranging species that now primarily
occurs in human-modified landscapes, some of which are rapidly
urbanising or subject to large-scale agricultural and mining
developments. Climate change is the major over-riding threat to
both northern and southern populations. These factors have already
been found to be associated/or responsible for *sic* several dramatic
declines in koala populations that have occurred in the northern
and western parts of its range (e.g. Gordon *et al.* 1988, Seabrook *et*

[xx] Out of a group of 20 experts, 18 were involved in one get together and 15 in
another. Fifteen of them, with two 'elicitators' wrote another paper about it.
Thirteen of them were amongst the 17 experts mentioned by the 18 authors of
this paper. Dr. Greg Gordon was the only expert amongst 20 who didn't co-
author one or another of the two journal articles about population crashes. He was
the only one who had attended the meeting of 43 scientists at Taronga Zoo four
decades earlier, when there were "large growing populations" i.e. irruptions.

al. 2011, Lunney et al. 2012, 2017).

Paragraph 9: This merely restates the experts' argument which ignores the major part of the ecological history of the koala. This is why I submitted the letter. The response did not address this. They stated that they were 17 experts - I can only assume that one author does not claim expertise. They restate the claim that climate change is the main threat to koalas and cite Lunney's paper, seemingly contradicting their Paragraph 6.

This correspondent's letter challenges these conclusions. It asserts that "conserving koalas should be easy". The central tenet of the article is that "Koalas were naturally rare and have repeatedly irrupted and declined at different times and places since Europeans occupied Australia." This tenet is fundamentally flawed. That koala populations are irruptive is remarkably naïve. It is based on anecdotal observations based on the recollections of individual residents, none of which are supported by rigorous data from the modern era. The koala no longer lives in a pre-European landscape. Furthermore, it is hard to reconcile "irruptive" with known koala fecundity[xxi] – even in a disease-free environment.

Paragraph 10: The central tenet of my letter is an historical fact that is fully evident in my primary reference. It does not rely on anybody's recollections. Five of the experts have published articles discussing reasons for historical irruptions of koalas (Melzer et al. 2000; Lunney et al. 2010; Close et al. 2015). These are discussed in my primary reference. My letter cites "rigorous modern data" presented by some of the experts, demonstrating irruptions that have been inaccurately described as recoveries.

Having an historical view to managing koala populations in the future based on a misguided interpretation of the past is neither sensible nor possible. In recent decades, urban development, linear infrastructure and mining became more extensive and intensive, and the environmental impacts of climate change have intensified greatly. Consequently, it is necessary to review the status and ecological outlook of the koala under these contemporary

---

[xxi] I have since found that one of the experts (Menkhorst 2008) has previously stated that koalas are "highly fecund" and populations may "double every three years"

conditions.

Paragraph 11: My letter discusses contemporary irruptions and declines to the maximum extent possible in 800 words.

The author 'cherry picks' supposed flaws in our paper but fails to provide any alternative credible science. The correspondent claims that koalas are not under threat. It argues *sic* conservation managers should focus on reinstating mild fire regimes to maintain healthy and diverse ecosystems with low densities of koalas in reserves and higher, but sustainable densities in multiple-use forests. The increasing intensity of climate change is making opportunities to complete mild fire management[xxii] more difficult. The Victorian Government is struggling to meet its fuel reduction requirements due to difficulty in finding the right conditions in which to reduce fuel by the required amount. The opportunities to manage koala populations through reintroducing mild fire are becoming very difficult if not impossible. It is an incredibly naïve notion that koala populations can be managed this way. Further, what are sustainable densities and how are they to be maintained as the author asserts that koala populations in the right conditions are irruptive?

Paragraph 12: Fire management is a big issue that cannot possibly be addressed in the same 800 word letter. History shows that it can be done. I addressed the issue of sustainable densities of koalas in the full paper that you rejected as being outside the scope of the journal. I cannot do it in an 800 word letter.

In conclusion, our firm response to this correspondent's letter is that it is not worthy of publication. It does not provide any scientific basis but merely uninformed opinion, and seeks to undermine the bigger picture of koala and wildlife conservation in rapidly changing human landscapes.

In addition, we think this is a terrible way for science to progress – i.e. letter writing that contains no data and is not peer reviewed. The author gets a 'publication' and his/her ideas out there without having to go through the same level of rigour as everyone else.

Paragraphs 13 and 14: The scientific basis is in my first three

---

[xxii] Mild fire management can never be 'completed', it must be ongoing as it was for 40,000 years before whitefellas disrupted it.

references of the 5 allowed. The other two references put the experts' case. I cannot do any better within the specifications of an 800 word letter. You did not send my full paper out for review because it was supposedly outside the scope of the journal.

We add that, in our view, editorial policy that does not disclose the author's name, as in this case, creates a bias in that the correspondent knew our names and could, for example, select other of our publications to criticise, but the policy denies us that option. When reviewing a paper, we accept the journal's policy of not disclosing the author's name, but this is a debate, not a review, and we ask for this policy to be reconsidered.

Paragraph 15: This seems to be rather cynical ... I am well acquainted with 5 of the experts and have met several others. Daniel Lunney and others published this about me [in their previously discussed *Rebuttal*]: "**A personal point of view** ... Part of this view is that koala habitat is best managed with logging and mild fire". *Please refer to their second paragraph. No-one else has published a comprehensive review of the koala's history across its range. They should know it is my letter.*

Clive McAlpine
Daniel Lunney
Christine Adams-Hosking
Alistair Melzer
Peter Menkhorst
Stephen Phillips
David Phalen
William Ellis
William Foley
Greg Baxter
Deidre de Villiers
Rodney Kavanagh
Charles Todd
Desley Whisson
Robyn Molsher
Michele Walter
Ivan Lawler
Robert Close

So my full discussion was rejected because it was outside the scope of the journal, and my letter was rejected because it was not a full discussion. Obviously, there was little point in submitting the second letter I had prepared, commenting on another article in *Biological Conservation*. Here it is:

Disease does not cause koala decline: Comment on an article by Grogan et al.

Grogan et al. (2018) presented a framework for evaluating the role of disease in species decline, illustrating it by reference to koalas. They found evidence that Chlamydia can be a major cause of morbidity, sterility and mortality of koalas, but not of population declines. They concluded that its importance as a driver of population dynamics may differ across the koala's range. I argue that native pathogens cannot be drivers of species decline.

Koalas have repeatedly irrupted in chronically declining eucalypt ecosystems and then declined during major droughts. Declining eucalypts provide a temporary abundance of soft, juicy and nutritious food in resprouting foliage until the trees' reserves are exhausted (see Jurskis 2017). Koala declines sometimes involve predators and pathogens. In other situations, decline has been attributed to 'overbrowsing'.

Chlamydiosis was diagnosed in a high proportion of necropsies from peri-urban populations. Grogan et al. suggested this would be unexpected of an opportunistic pathogen infecting stressed animals. Supposedly Chlamydia "are never innocuous commensals"[xxiii] *because they are obligate intracellular pathogens. However, disease or predation has not impacted the very few low-density koala populations that have been studied intensively.*

Sparse populations survived unscathed through major droughts during two centuries since European occupation of Australia. In contrast, dense populations crashed during each extreme event. The role of chlamydiosis in decline of koalas has been misinterpreted because the great majority of ecological studies have occurred in unsustainably dense populations which are inevitably stressed by malnutrition exacerbated by drought.

For example, when Europeans occupied the Bega Valley in 1830 they did not see koalas. During the 1860s, koalas irrupted,

---

[xxiii] species living in close association, such that one species benefits without harming the other.

reaching plague proportions by 1880. A disease epidemic affected koalas around 1905, then koalas declined precipitously and disappeared by the time that peak of the Federation Drought occurred in 1909 (Lunney and Leary 1988). A very low-density population persisted in the surrounding forests. The "gold standard" *ELISA test (Grogan et al.) showed that it is infected by chlamydia, but there is no expression of disease. This population persisted, and a subset northeast of Bega increased, through the Millennium Drought.*

A dense population of koalas at Cape Otway continued to irrupt during and after the drought. About 700 starving koalas were destroyed in 2013/14. During the following two years 450 females received fertility control implants, 43 were culled, 4 dependent young were placed in zoological parks, and 647 adults as well as 74 dependent young were translocated to nearby forests. By late 2016, there were still too many koalas, and "further actions" *were required to control* "over-browsing" *(DELWP 2016).*

Browsing by dense populations exacerbates tree decline, even when fecundity is suppressed by chlamydiosis, because survival of juveniles increases as fertility declines (Grogan et al.). Koalas at Cape Otway would have inevitably declined as mortality of trees and koalas increased in the absence of culling, sterilisation and translocation. It makes no difference whether malnourished koalas succumb to predators, disease or starvation, the fundamental cause of population decline is shortage of food.

Wide-ranging longitudinal studies and gold standard diagnostics as recommended by Grogan et al. will not change this conclusion. A wealth of empirical evidence confirms the basic ecological tenet of the trophic ziggurat. When the base of the ziggurat increases, successive levels increase in turn. When the base contracts, higher levels can over-run their food resources and seem to be controlling them from above. However, top-heavy structures inevitably topple.

Pathological studies may lead to improved animal welfare, but they cannot assist wildlife conservation because they occur long after the real cause of population decline has already had an effect. In the case of koalas, the cause is lack of mild burning and the initial effect is irruption of koalas in chronically declining trees. Grogan et al. noted that severe symptoms of chlamydiosis may take years to manifest and so be masked by unrelated mortality in populations of young average age. If so, disease is not a conservation issue.

Studies of chlamydiosis are a distraction from biological conservation because whole ecosystems are adversely affected by lack of mild burning. A specialised reductionist approach diverts attention from the big picture. New South Wales is expending large amounts on research, including pathology, of koala declines and on aetiology [the way it comes to pass] *of so-called bell miner associated dieback (BMAD) of eucalypts. Lack of mild burning causes both problems in the same forests.*

In the absence of holistic ecology, governments have been persuaded that Chlamydia causes koala decline, and bellbirds cause irruptions of psyllids leading to eucalypt decline. Policy aims to reduce chlamydia, psyllids and bellbirds and increase koalas. In fact, irruptions of koalas can lead to chlamydiosis, whilst irruptions of psyllids can lead to irruptions of bellbirds.

Conservation of all species, including the dominant eucalypts in many endangered ecological communities, depends upon reintroduction of mild fire to restore resilience and biodiversity.

References

Grogan, L.F., Peel, A.J., Kerlin, D., Ellis, W., Jones, D., Hero, J.-M., McCallum, H., 2018. Is disease a major causal factor in declines? An Evidence Framework and case study on koala chlamydiosis. Biological Conservation 221, 334-344.

Jurskis, V., 2017. Ecological history of the koala and implications for management. Wildlife Research 44, 471-483.

Lunney, D., and Leary, T., 1988. The impact on native mammals of land-use changes and exotic species in the Bega district, New South Wales, since settlement. Australian Journal of Ecology 13, 67–92.

Department of Environment, Land, Water and Planning, 2016. Koalas at Cape Otway. The State of Victoria https://www.wildlife.vic.gov.au/our-wildlife/koalas/koalas-at-cape-otway

Having decided not to waste my time submitting this letter to the Journal, I sent a copy to the senior author Dr. Grogan, requesting her comments. I received no reply. I note that one of her co-authors, Dr. Ellis, was also one of the 18 authors/17 experts who seem to have persuaded the Chief Editor not to publish my other letter. He was previously attached to San Diego Zoo, which seems to have difficulties with some historical facts about koalas (Introduction).

The *Geographic Citizen Science* paper promoting ineffective survey techniques was also published by *Biological Conservation*, and two of its authors were the two leading authors out of the 17.5 experts. They seem to have the game pretty well sewn up.

I think that some current terminology, such as *peer-reviewed*, *scientific consensus* and *independent expert*, used rather freely to gain public confidence, should be ringing alarm bells.

Notes

1   Adams-Hosking *et al.* 2016

2   Lunney *et al.* 2014

3   Reed *et al.* 1990

4   Bergin 1978 p. v

5   Lunney *et al.* 1997

6   NSW Government 1996

7   Jurskis and Potter 1997

8   Cook 1993

9   Griffith *et al.* 2013

10 Allen 1995

11 Jurskis *et al.* 2001

12 Jurskis 2017a pp. 476-478

13 Jurskis 2002

14 Lunney and Leary 1988

15 Reed and Lunney 1990

16 DECCW 2010

17 Lunney *et al.* 2014

18 Lunney and Barker 1986/7

19 Kavanagh *et al.* 1995

20 OEH 2016

21 Jurskis *et al.* 2001 Table 1

22 Lunney *et al.* 2009 Fig 9

23 DECCW 2010 Fig 1

24 Lunney *et al.* 2017a pp. 454, 456

25 Speakman and Blair 2016

26 Predavec 2016

27 Law *et al*. 2019
28 Lunney *et al*. 2010
29 Tilley and Uebel 1990
30 Close *et al*. 2015
31 Pringle *et al*. 2009
32 Lunney *et al*. 2016a
33 Lunney *et al*. 2009
34 Lunney *et al*. 2016b
35 State Forests 1995
36 Calaby 1966
37 Jurskis 2005
38 Smith and Ximenes 2019 p. 38
39 J. Black, Forestry Corporation pers. comm.
40 Law *et al*. 2018
41 Brown *et al*. 2018
42 Rennison 2017
43 McAlpine *et al*. 2015
44 Jurskis 2017a
45 Beyer *et al*. 2018

5

FAIRDINKUM SCIENCE

Once upon a time, we might have viewed climate sceptics as
merely frustrating... But it's 2019, and now we know better.

Misha Ketchell – Editor and Executive Director,
The Conversation

Here is some of *the conversation* in which academia apparently
doesn't wish to engage:

History of the Koala Coast

European exploration commenced with a two-day visit by
Matthew Flinders in 1799. Surveyor General Oxley explored
the area twice over 11 days in 1823 and 1824. He rescued two
shipwrecked sailors who had lived with Aborigines for seven
months and described their culture, including fighting, funerals,
hunting, gathering and fishing. A penal colony was established
at Redcliffe in 1824 and moved to Brisbane in 1825. Convicts
were employed in farming, grazing, timbergetting and mining.
Extensive explorations of the district were made by Captain
Logan, Majors Lockyer and Cotton, Foreman Petrie and Botanist
Allan Cunningham. Detailed trigonometric survey was carried
out before the first land sales in 1842. No reports of koalas
derive from any of these sources.[1,2]

Naturalist John Gould published the first reference to koalas.[3]
He never visited the area, but his collector, John Gilbert, arrived
at the nearby Darling Downs in 1844, whence he set off with
Leichardt's Expedition. Six other members of the expedition
sailed to Moreton Bay before travelling to the Darling Downs.

It seems likely, from Gould's reference, that Gilbert either saw a koala in brush on the coastal escarpment of The Downs, or was informed of such a sighting by another member of the party. Gilbert wrote to Gould before he departed from The Downs, and was killed by Aborigines[xxiv] near the Gulf of Carpentaria in 1845.

As a small boy, around 1890, Thomas Hardcastle witnessed a corroboree[xxv] at his grandfather's property near Boonah, on the southwestern margin of the Koala Coast, where he saw *"heaps of wallabies, paddymelons, possums, native bears, etc., being prepared for cooking"*.[4] In 1904 Howitt reported information from James Gibson that newly initiated young Aboriginal men of the coastal Chepara Tribe or Jeeparra Clan were allowed to eat *"kangaroo, male opossum, native bear, and honey"* in their probationary period. During this time they were *"practically placed in a state of privation, while being possibly surrounded by plentiful but forbidden food"*.[4,5] The implication is that koalas were hard to catch. Apart from these references, koalas were not reported at Moreton Bay prior to 1900, when they suddenly became abundant.[6] Evidently they irrupted in the late 19th Century.

After that, their abundance mostly varied with rainfall.[6]

The first ecological study of koalas in this region was conducted in 1987/88 when they apparently increased after native pastures were initially alienated for future residential development. Their density (0.4 per ha) was reported to be relatively low in a wider context, but typical of southeastern QLD. Koalas were easily visible. There were moderate rates of predation and disease. The fertility rate was 67%, and 12% of the population had clinical symptoms of disease (chlamydiosis). Eight percent of radio-collared koalas died of natural causes over the year of the study. One suffered accidental trauma, one predation, and the rest

---

[xxiv] Apparently in retribution for sexual assaults by the expedition's guides on local Aboriginal women[6]

[xxv] A formal gathering of Aboriginal groups from a broad region, involving ritual, dancing and celebration

disease.[7]

Previous ecological studies of koalas had been restricted to high-density populations of one or more koalas per hectare in supposed high-quality habitats. The first study recognising that koalas are naturally widespread at low densities, in what were previously thought to be poor-quality habitats, was reported from two sites in central QLD in 1994. Home ranges averaged about 67 and 210 hectares. Corresponding densities were 0.01 and 0.005 koalas per hectare.[8] Our radio-tracking study at Eden was the first detailed ecological study of a natural, low-density population. The density on the Koala Coast was 70 times greater, while other studies had reported up to 1300 times higher densities.[9]

The Koala Coast population was considered to be *"relatively secure"* at this time, but declined by 75% between 1996 and 2012[10], coincident with the Millennium Drought from 1997 to 2009, and record floods in 2010 and 2011.[11] During this period, population densities in the region varied from 0.8 to < 0.1 koalas per hectare, and the steepest declines apparently occurred in the sub-populations having the highest initial densities. The rate of decline flattened after drought-break. Average densities in bushland and urban areas were ~ 0.1 koalas per ha in 2012.[12]

Between 1997 and 2013, more than 20,000 koalas were submitted to veterinary hospitals in the region. Fifty-two percent were diseased, 16% had suffered road accident trauma and 14% were wasting. However, vehicle injuries declined from ~ 30% to ~ 10% whilst wasting increased from ~ 3% of submissions in 1997 to ~ 20% by 2013.[13] Pathologists found strong evidence for *Chlamydia pecorum* as a major cause of morbidity, sterility and mortality, but not of population declines. They found no evidence for chlamydiosis as a symptom of habitat loss through urbanisation. They apparently did not consider any evidence for chlamydiosis as a symptom of malnutrition.[14]

Wasting as a proportion of total hospital admissions increased roughly six-fold during the drought. Food for koalas dwindled, but starving koalas continued to feed predators and diseases. The results of radio-tracking studies before and after the drought suggest that the overall mortality rate nearly doubled. Meanwhile, in central QLD, very low-density populations persisted in what were supposed to be poor quality habitats. At the same time, dense populations in supposedly high quality riparian habitats suffered severe decline or local extinction.[15] For example, numbers crashed in pastoral holdings around Minerva Hills National Park, whereas koalas persisted in the park at densities of 0.02 per hectare.[16]

On the Koala Coast, between 2009 and 2014, 180 koalas were moved out of the way to allow construction of a shopping centre at Coomera. Forty two percent died in their new habitat. Of the animals which weren't moved because they weren't in the way, fifty percent died. Queensland's Environment Minister said that both groups were threatened by habitat loss, predation, road trauma and disease, so translocation wasn't the problem.[17]

Ecologists controlled wild dogs and disease in another sub-population, from 2013 to 2017, whilst 62 hectares of bush were being cleared for a railway. Five hundred and three koalas were captured and tracked.[18] Obviously the study area was much larger than the clearing area, but the scientists didn't tell us the area. There was an extraordinarily high density of wild dogs and a high rate of predation after koala densities had apparently doubled (from 0.4 to 0.8 per hectare) at some sites before crashing to ~ 0.1 in the drought.[7,10,12] Forty-one wild dogs were destroyed.

There were 144 confirmed predations of koalas, 81% by wild dogs, 15% by carpet snakes (a native python) and 4% by domestic dogs. Population density was ~ 0.2 koalas per hectare. There was 15% annual mortality of adult koalas; 63% by predation, 29% by disease and 3% by road accident trauma. Population growth rates were 0.7, 0.9, 1.1 and 1.2 over each of the four years respectively.[18]

While their food trees were partially recovering after drought-breaking rains, treatment of chlamydiosis and destruction of wild dogs obviously had some benefits for koalas. Not all cases of disease or trauma were treatable, so some koalas were euthanased. However, there were no benefits for species conservation, since koalas remained in unsustainably high densities and the population growth rate was 1.2 in the final year of the study. This is clearly unsustainable. If it were maintained, the population would double within four years. Realistically, the rate would increase. A fundamental problem with managing iconic species is the assumption that more is better.

High mortality of koalas in QLD during the 1920s was attributed mainly to overly dense populations, drought, disease and predation by dingoes and foxes.[19] Predation, disease or drought has not adversely impacted the very few low-density koala populations that have been studied intensively, for example at Eden and Campbelltown where two sub-populations continued to increase during the Millennium Drought. Substantial levels of disease, predation and/or road trauma are consequences of unsustainably dense populations. Radio-collared koalas at Campbelltown occupying home ranges that included roads and domestic dogs lived long lives and died of natural causes.[20] In any case, experience on the Koala Coast indicates that motor vehicle trauma can be substantially reduced by traffic management.

Defoliation of trees and/or decline of koala populations have occurred wherever reported densities were 0.1 per ha or higher.[21] Crashes of high-density populations are inevitable after they reach unsustainable numbers in response to a temporary surplus of food. These are usually precipitated by drought, when declining trees are no longer able to maintain a continuous turnover of new shoots. Low-density koala populations are resilient because healthy trees suddenly faced with acute stress have considerable nutrient reserves. Chronically declining trees quickly exhaust their depleted reserves and succumb to drought stress.

The pre-European range of the koala

John Gould wrote the first description of the koala's distribution (as it was known in 1844)[3]:

> ... *this remarkable creature is only found in the south-eastern portion ... It is in the brushes which skirt the sea side of the mountain-ranges between the district of Illawarra and the River Clarence* [NSW coast] *that it is most numerous ...*

> ... *a portion of my time and attention was directed to the fauna of the dense and luxuriant brushes which stretch along the south-eastern coast, from Illawarra to Moreton Bay* [QLD]. *I also spent some time among the cedar brushes of the mountain ranges of the interior, particularly those bordering the well-known Liverpool Plains* [NSW Murray-Darling Basin]. *In all these localities the koala is to be found ... although nowhere very abundant ... without the aid of the natives, its presence ... can rarely be detected.*

Historical records assembled by Bill Gammage show that the koala was associated with dense, scrubby forests in "*distinct, lightly populated and few*" locations. As European settlement progressed, "*Within a few decades koalas were a plague*".[22] Although the timing varied, the irruptions were very widespread. Modern descriptions of the koala's original range are based on its visible distribution at the height of irruptions. For example Fred Lewis, in 1934, used 1889 as his baseline for VIC.[23] The baseline used for northern QLD is the 1920s and 30s.[24] The baseline for SA is a guesstimate made in 1924 for the "*early days of settlement*" which commenced in 1837. So it can be no earlier than about 1870, when koalas were "*by no means uncommon in certain districts*" of the southeast.[25]

Figure 2 shows, on the left, the estimated range of the koala at the height of the early irruptions compared to, on the right, the range of visible populations in 1934. The draftsman was Noel Burnet who opened Sydney's Koala Park in 1930. It is noteworthy that even this large 'range' falls short of encompassing the entire perimeter within which koalas have been found. For example, in 1930 there was a sighting hundreds of kilometres north of any others, at the bottom of Cape York Peninsula near Cooktown.[26]

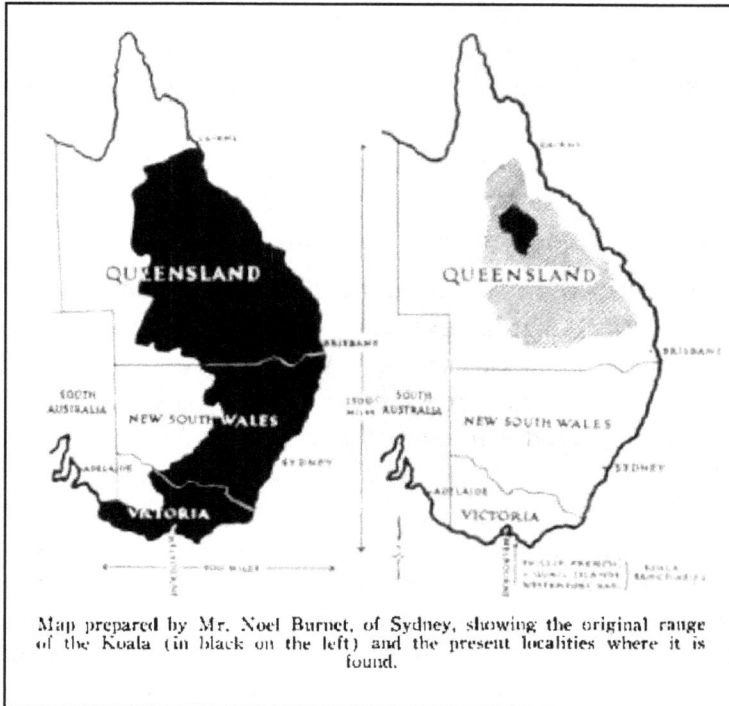

Map prepared by Mr. Noel Burnet, of Sydney, showing the original range of the Koala (in black on the left) and the present localities where it is found.

Fig. 2: Reproduced from *The Victorian Naturalist*, courtesy of FNCV

Having had the rare privilege of studying a natural, low density koala population, I was taken aback when Phil Cheney asked me *where did all these irruptions come from?*. The inescapable conclusion from consideration of radio-tracking studies of naturally sparse populations in the context of the historical records, is that koala habitats were not *distinct* and *few*, but they were indeed very *lightly populated*. There were actually a few distinct, more heavily populated areas as identified by Strzelecki and Gould, and later by Gammage.

The records noted by Gammage, Gould and Strzelecki, all came from areas of very poor visibility and with assistance from Aboriginal people. In the case of the former two sources, it is obvious that blackfellas knew the koalas were there and protected the brushes and scrubs by mild burning around their margins. In the latter case, Strzelecki's Aboriginal guide Charley Tarra clearly knew to look for koalas in the dense scrubby forest. Explorers and pioneers didn't see koalas where they would have been highly visible, in the open riparian woodlands now considered to be prime habitats, because they weren't there. The reason koalas were able to occupy these areas in large numbers within a few decades of European development is that they were widespread and fecund.

A reasonable representation of the koala's natural range would be the original extent of eucalypt forest east of a line from the head of the Gulf of St. Vincent in SA to the mouth of the Endeavour River at Cooktown in far northern QLD. Interspersed amongst this natural habitat, which has mostly been retained as forest, were the grassy woodlands of the Brigalow Belt, which didn't support koalas. These woodlands apparently developed into forests and scrubs after Aboriginal management was affected by the first smallpox epidemic, likely introduced by Macassan trepangers in the 1780s.[27] Some of this new habitat has since been cleared. Some originally grassy woodlands developed into the Pilliga Scrub after pastoralists disrupted Aboriginal burning. The eucalypt plantations of the Green Triangle around the SA/VIC border represent a recent increase in koala habitat. These historical and ongoing changes are of no consequence to the conservation of the species.

Unrecognised irruptions

The Pilliga koalas had irrupted from *"exceptionally low numbers ... throughout most of the last century"* before they crashed, for a second time, during the Millennium Drought. The experts discussed possible reasons for the crash, but not for the dramatic irruption that preceded the crash.[28] The original irruption coincided with dense new growth of forest from 1878 in wet seasons after destocking and abandonment of pastoral holdings during drought.[29] The second irruption also coincided with a dramatic increase in young eucalypt foliage. Poisoning of eucalypts to promote cypress growth had been discontinued in 1972 and ringbarking of eucalypts was discontinued early in the 1980s. Also, harvesting of small or defective ironbark trees commenced when the Insultimber sawmill[xxvi] opened in 1975, and produced relatively dense coppice regeneration.[30]

Koalas are currently irrupting from Buchan to Mallacoota – Genoa (East Gippsland VIC), where they are easily visible in declining shrub-infested forests, and in the adjoining Eden region (NSW); also north of Mansfield (central VIC) where Vicroads has seen the need to erect warning signs.[21] These irruptions were not identified by the experts. Similarly, the current unrecognised irruption around Campbelltown south of Sydney has been noticed 15 kilometres to the east-northeast at Lucas Heights, where a koala turned up in a eucalypt plantation at the nuclear reactor facility in 2017, and the RTA has recently erected warning signs on the main road through declining forest (Figure 3).

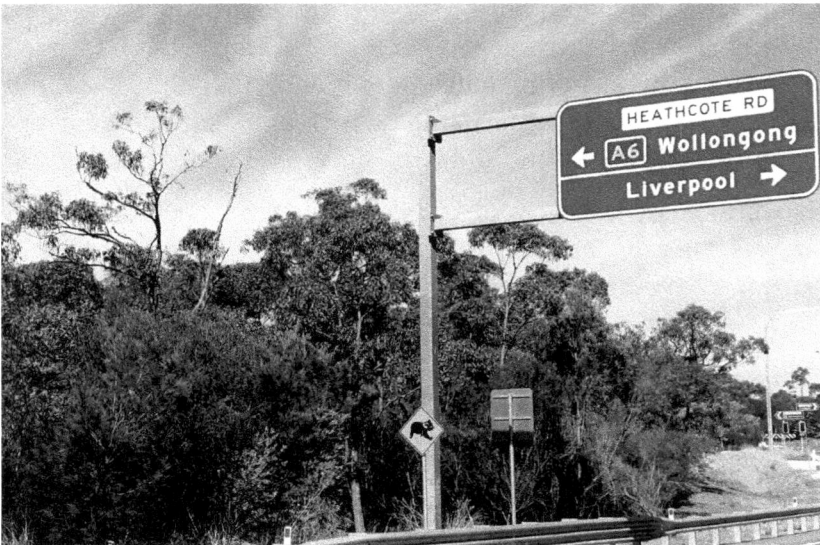

Fig 3. Sign of a koala irruption in dense scrubby forest on Sydney's southern outskirts. Photo by the Author.

[xxvi] The mill produced fence posts and droppers for electric fences, using eco-friendly natural insulation.

North versus south

The difference between the supposedly threatened koalas in QLD, NSW and ACT compared to the *overabundant* koalas in VIC and SA, is an historical accident rather than an ecological dilemma. The difference is simply in timing and reporting of irruptions. Koalas in the south irrupted before there was any clearing for pastoral development. They firstly irrupted in the Strzeleckis before European settlement. Secondly, they irrupted on Wilson's Promontory after bush grazing was stopped and the area was declared a National Park in 1908.[31]

This was the first documented case where so-called overbrowsing by koalas killed trees. Despite the opinions of our, say seventeen and a half, koala experts, it had nothing to do with genetic bottlenecks and reintroductions or absence of disease and/or predators. The Victorian Field Naturalists surveyed The Prom in 1905. Koalas were one of few native animals they found. The area was undeveloped, densely timbered and visited only by cattle musterers and, in winter, by koala-skin hunters.[31] Apparently The Prom had escaped the worst impacts of megafires around 1820, and in 1851 and 1898. The area was not dominated by impenetrable eucalypt sapling scrubs which would have prevented cattle grazing.

Nevertheless, koalas were superabundant in declining trees. It was *"not an unusual sight to see three or four of these harmless creatures, often one or more with a joey clinging to its mother's back, in a single tree"*. When grazing ceased following reservation of the area as a National Park in 1908, koalas *"became so numerous that in favourable situations one could always rely on seeing from 30 to 40 in a comparatively small area"*. Manna gums (*Eucalyptus viminalis*) started to die and koalas were culled. Manna gums resprouted and koalas flocked in to browse them. *"In certain localities"*, manna gum *"was practically exterminated"*. Koalas died or supposedly moved into blue gum (*E. globulus*) in the ranges. *"Several koalas were forwarded to New South Wales, South Australia and Western Australia"*.[31]

The photo on the front cover shows this same process in operation at Raymond Island today. Lack of mild burning or grazing in the reserve has led to tree decline, irruption of koalas and growth of dense scrub or bracken. Deborah Tabart OAM, Chief Executive Officer of AKF, has the story back to front, suggesting that burning and growth of bracken kills the trees[32]. The photo on the back cover shows that any tender new eucalypt shoots which escape being eaten by koalas are, later on, attacked by insects adapted to eating harder foliage.

After visible koala populations in VIC generally crashed during the Federation Drought, tens of thousands of koalas from artificial island populations were 'reintroduced' into supposedly unoccupied mainland habitats over the best part of a century from 1923. The release sites were 'protected' from fire[33], so trees started to decline and koalas irrupted. In 1981, 75 koalas were translocated from French Island to Cape Otway. Within 20 years, koalas had irrupted at the Cape. The population didn't crash during the Millennium Drought, despite some animals suffering starvation. After the drought, it continued to increase, reaching densities of 20 per hectare by 2013. This is 2000 to 4000 times the density of resilient populations in central QLD and southern NSW. Fifteen of 21 radio-collared koalas starved to death or were euthenased by the end of that year.[34]

One of our 17.5 koala experts was in charge of this study. When I had the temerity to challenge the pronouncements on so-called overbrowsing, Dr. Desley Whisson quickly 'put me in my place':

> In fact it is very simple. Koalas from a genetically-poor population are introduced to a highly preferred food source (manna gum), their numbers increase in the absence of natural regulators to the point where their trees die and the koalas starve. ...
>
> The answer to koala overabundance is quite simple: reduce the koala population and trees become healthy again.[35]

Irruptions have also occurred in new eucalypt plantings,

whether for amenity, such as around Gunnedah NSW, or for timber, such as in the Green Triangle of VIC/SA. These koalas were not introduced. Koalas around Gunnedah suffered a severe decline, whilst koalas in the Green Triangle underwent a *"managed decline"*, during the Millennium Drought.[7] Dense koala populations in industrial blue gum plantations in the Green Triangle and in South Gippsland pose animal welfare and operational problems for plantation owners and government.[36,37]

Increasing populations are not consequences of inbreeding or absence of diseases and predators. Predators and diseases can increase after koalas irrupt. Young koalas trying to disperse are a boon for predators. Malnourished koalas can support disease epidemics. For example, in The Pilliga, foxes became abundant and preyed on koalas around 1910, after they had irrupted and a skin industry had established. Koalas were afflicted by disease at the same time, and the population crashed during droughts around the time of the First World War.[28,29] Historical and modern irruptions of koalas in NSW and QLD have gone unrecognised and unreported.

Arbivores, predators and diseases increase when their food increases, and decline when their food inevitably declines. The only *natural regulator* of koalas or any other animal is food. Dr. Whisson and colleagues were tracking koalas at Cape Otway when a crash commenced. They suggested that strong *site fidelity* prevented starving koalas from moving into alternative, less preferred habitats. However, six koalas survived by moving as much as 500 metres to small isolated patches of manna gum that were not completely defoliated.

It seems that other *"less preferred habitats"* were either not suitable habitats, or more likely were already occupied to the limit of their much smaller carrying capacities. Starving mothers abandoned their dependent young. There was no alternative, unutilised food source; if there had been, starving koalas would have eaten it. For example, in South Gippsland, koalas in plague populations around 1877 fed on new pastures as did plagues of caterpillars.[38] In *Blinky Bill*, Dorothy Wall wrote: *"Occasionally one* ['bear'] *will come down to feed on some vegetation in the grass".*[39]

When I was editing this chapter in spring 2019, cattleman Chris Commins called in on his way back from Bega (Far South Coast NSW) with a quarter-tonne of snail bait to save his new pasture at Wingan River in East Gippsland (VIC). Birds and blue tongue lizards couldn't breed fast enough to take advantage of the irruption of snails that were taking advantage of the new food resource. Chris's daughter Emma measured some transects and found that there were 2.6 million of these small conical snails per hectare of pasture.

The irrupting, supposedly reintroduced koala population at Cape Otway is the least inbred of seven natural populations, stretching as far north as the central QLD coast. There is no difference in genetic diversity between koalas at the Cape and those in the supposed original source population of South Gippsland.[40] A genuinely artificial population from St. Bees Island north of St. Lawrence in QLD has the highest genetic diversity whilst the Koala Coast population is the most inbred.[41]

There is as much genetic similarity amongst animals on the Koala Coast as in the famously inbred French Island population, supposedly the source of most of today's Victorian koalas.[41,42] It seems the experts may have got the genetics back to front, as well as the basic ecology. Koalas have equal or better genetic diversity than large wild populations such as feral pigs in Europe or wolves in North America. Amongst recognised natural koala populations across the range, the Koala Coast population, which was not introduced, but irrupted from a low base in the 1980s, is more inbred, and is disease prone.[41]

However, it makes no difference to conservation of the species whether unsustainably dense populations mostly succumb to disease or starvation. Koalas would have crashed as trees died at Cape Otway, had they not been euthenased, sterilised and/or translocated. It all comes back to carrying capacity.

Translocation

Drought-stricken graziers know that once their livestock have eaten what they can, there's no point in putting them in with other stock that still have a bit of feed in another paddock. That's why they feed them, drove them through the *long paddock*, sell them for next to nothing or shoot them. Koala experts are apparently smarter. They look for an 'empty' paddock. Unfortunately for koalas and trees, there's no such thing in nature. Translocation doesn't work. The problem of limited carrying capacity can be hidden if 'excess' koalas are distributed in large areas of low carrying capacity where irruptions are unlikely. The inevitable consequence must be malnutrition and lingering death of less competitive koalas, whether local or introduced. Alternatively, translocation can speed the demise of unsustainably dense populations.

For example 47% (25/53) of Victorian koalas experimentally translocated in 1983, suffered disease (contracted from local koalas), declined in condition, disappeared and/or died in less than two years.[43] The experts seemingly learnt nothing from the experiment. Over 10 years after 1997, more than 3,000 koalas from Kangaroo Island were sterilised and released in mainland SA at a density of one koala per hectare.[44] Thirty eight percent of them (that's more than 1,100 koalas) died within a year, leaving, with koalas that were already there, up to one koala per 2.5 hectares (0.4 koalas per hectare)—an unsustainable density as proven on the koala Coast. The experts claimed that none of the local koalas died. Perhaps not in the short term. Remember that 42% of koalas moved from the Coomera shopping centre development died in their new home and 50% of the overcrowded koalas that weren't moved perished in their old home.

Mr. Menkhorst and Dr. Whisson were involved in a study of translocating 36 koalas from Cape Otway to habitat near Benwerrin VIC, which was already occupied by at least one koala per thirty hectares (0.03 koalas per hectare). Even though 25% died or disappeared within a year, and the mortality rate was the same as that for the remaining koalas at the Cape, they proposed more translocations.[45] This recommendation was published by *Wildlife Research*.

When koalas were translocated from Campbelltown near Sydney, 100 km south into supposedly unoccupied habitat, local koalas appeared. One made a genetic contribution to an offspring of an introduced koala. Although no koalas had been seen in the area for 30 years, there was clearly a low-density breeding population.[20] This is part of a population that extends from the Hunter Valley in NSW to VIC, where irruptions are occurring in long-unburnt chronically declining forests in East Gippsland.[20,21] (Most of these forests were incinerated by megafires around New Year's Day 2020. See Postscript).

Carrying Capacity or Sustainable Density

Koala densities of 0.1 per ha and higher have been regarded as moderate and sustainable[21,46] or even as low.[7,16] History shows that these are unnaturally high densities, and that dense populations have repeatedly crashed during droughts. Ecologists studying dense populations have been unable to recognise early stages of eucalypt decline, as have those studying the parallel problem of psyllid irruptions.[20,21,47] So-called overbrowsing by koalas and 'BMAD' are end stages of chronic eucalypt decline in the absence of mild burning.

Burning and/or grazing of native pastures maintains sunny, airy, warm and dry topsoils and natural nutrient cycling processes which support mature trees, herbs and grasses. In the absence of burning and/or grazing, soil physics and chemistry change and vegetation responds, reinforcing the changes. Mulch builds up, sunshine and air circulation are reduced. Nitrogen in litter, seedlings and herbage that had previously been volatilised by fires and returned to the atmosphere, or mineralised by fires and taken up by the flush of new growth, now accumulates in the soil and the developing shrubbery.[48]

Topsoils become cooler, damper, softer and deeper. Carbon to Nitrogen ratios of soils are reduced, acid soils become more acid and microtoxins such as aluminium and manganese are released. These inhibit tree roots and mycorrhizae. They become more susceptible to droughts and root rots such as phytophthora. The deteriorating soils and roots cause nutrient imbalances, particularly in ratios of Nitrogen to Phosphorus, and physiological changes in the trees. Their sapstreams and foliage become more attractive and nutritious to arbivores— that is anything that derives nutrients from any part of the tree including roots, sapwood, sap and leaves.[48,49,50]

Scientists from OEH and Australian National University,[47] seemingly without knowing, studied the nutritional value of eucalypt foliage from chronically declining trees near Bega. One of these scientists was from the ubiquitous 17.5. They suggested that koalas from this *"extremely low density"* irrupting population might spread into supposedly unoccupied parts of the forest if alleged threats from clearing, logging and climate change were *"controlled"*. Similarly, experts from UWS and Sydney University, including two others of the 17.5[20], predicted that koalas near Sydney *"will continue to increase in number and distribution until all suitable female home-ranges are occupied"*.

These ecologists apparently haven't recognised that koalas are increasing in response to temporarily increasing food supplies in dense regrowth forest arising from intensive harvesting and wildfires around 1980 near Bega and wildfires in 1977 near Campbelltown. In both areas, there is accelerated leaf-turnover in trees that are declining as a result of absence of mild burning and/or grazing.[21,48,51,52]

The density of the resilient koala population at Eden is in the order of 0.006 animals per hectare[53], very similar to resilient populations in central QLD.[8,15] The irrupting sub-population at Mumbulla is at least ten times this density, i.e. > 0.06. Male koalas were recently detected there at 88% of survey sites, compared to 64% of north coast sites.[54,55] The irrupting sub-population at Campbelltown – Lucas Heights reached ~ 0.03 animals per hectare near Campbelltown several years ago, similar to irrupting north coast populations. Researchers speculated that the population extending south through continuous forest to Eden and East Gippsland may have a density in the order of 0.01 animals per hectare.[20,56] The population in Minerva Hills National Park QLD persisted through the Millenium Drought at a density of 0.02[16], but it is not clear whether this population is irrupting. High density populations in riparian areas at Springsure crashed to 0.02 or less at the same time.[15]

Given the lack of studies in low-density populations, it can only be assumed that maximum sustainable densities of koalas in mature forests are probably around 0.01 animals per hectare, equivalent to an average home range area of around 100 hectares.[xxvii] If studies were conducted mainly in the virtually invisible, stable populations, it would be more immediately enlightening to refer to hectares per animal rather than animals per hectare. Credible estimates of populations through most of the koala's range could then be made simply as hectares of forest divided by average home range size. Thus, the supposedly extinct population at Eden probably numbered about 1200 animals[53] before irruptions commenced in the late 20th Century.

The great majority of ecological studies have occurred in irrupting or unsustainably dense populations of koalas, usually in riparian areas that are mostly not natural habitats. Increasing numbers of koalas have been misinterpreted as recoveries to presumed naturally high densities. Consequences of irruptions, such as lack of drought-tolerance, and high levels of predation, disease and trauma have been misinterpreted as causes of decline, whilst resilient low-density populations have been considered especially vulnerable to extinction. For example, the experts concluded that numbers of koalas were *"small but relatively stable"* near Sydney and the Southern Highlands, whilst the population extending south to Victoria was at *"critically low levels"*.[10]

[xxvii] A circle encompassing 100 hectares has a radius of 564 metres.

The 'scientific consensus' on koala ecology is totally flawed because it is based on unknowing observations of unsustainably dense populations of koalas in ecosystems lacking sustainable fire regimes (Chapter 1).

Notes

1   Field 1825
2   Craig 1925
3   Gould 1863
4   Steele 1984
5   Howitt 1904 pp. 583, 639
6   Gordon and Hrdina 2005
7   White and Kunst 1990
8   Melzer and Lamb 1994
9   Jurskis and Potter 1997 Table 19
10 McAlpine *et al.* 2015
11 South Eastern Australian Climate Initiative 2011
12 McAlpine *et al.* 2015 Fig. 2
13 Gonzalez-Astudillo *et al.* 2017 Table 1, Fig. 1
14 Grogan *et al.* 2018
15 Ellis *et al.* 2010
16 Anon. 2018 p. 144
17 Forbes and O'Brien 2018
18 Beyer *et al.* 2018
19 Gordon and Hrdina 2005 p. 78, Table 8
20 Close *et al.* 2015
21 Jurskis 2017a
22 Gammage 2011 pp. 197-199, 287-288
23 Lewis 1934 p. 73
24 Gordon and Hrdina Fig. 3
25 Robinson 1978
26 Gordon *et al.* 2006 p. 349
27 Jurskis 2015 pp. 73, 80-82
28 Lunney *et al.* 2017b
29 Rolls 1981 p. 183
30 van Kempen 1997
31 Kershaw 1934
32 Tabart 2019 p. 4

33 Menkhorst 2008

34 Whisson *et al.* 2016

35 Moore and Whisson 2015

36 Amis 2014

37 DELWP 2018

38 Coverdale 1920

39 Wall 1933

40 Wedrowicz *et al.* 2017 Figure 3

41 Kjeldsen 2016 Table 1

42 Jurskis and Potter 1997 Table 16

43 Lee *et al.* 1990

44 Whisson *et al.* 2012

45 Menkhorst *et al.* 2019

46 DELWP 2016

47 Stalenberg *et al.* 2014

48 Jurskis 2005

49 Turner *et al.* 2008

50 Dijkstra and Adams 2015

51 Jurskis *et al.* 2011

52 Tilley and Uebel 1990

53 Jurskis and Potter 1997 p. 32

54 Law *et al.* 2019

55 Law *et al.* 2018

56 Jurskis 2017a p. 474

6

GOVERNMENT WASTE

Freedom is the freedom to say that two plus two make four. If that is granted, all else follows.

Winston Smith in George Orwell's
Nineteen Eighty-Four, 1948

One of the koala experts, Mr. Peter Menkhorst, considers that:

> *Despite the cost and the threat of problems caused by reduced genetic variation, the re-establishment of the Koala in almost all remaining habitat across most of its original Victorian distribution can be considered the most successful wildlife management program undertaken in that State. It can also reasonably be claimed to be a successful threatened species recovery program, one of very few ever achieved in Victoria*

> *... However, neither the animal welfare cost, nor the financial cost, was ever adequately documented, and the genetic cost is, perhaps, yet to become clear.*[1]

NSW and QLD probably haven't spent nearly as much on research and seeming mismanagement of koalas. The relevant experts in the north don't claim credit for the secondary irruptions that they describe as *recovery* rather than *re-establishment*. At the same time, the recent inevitable crashes of unsustainably dense populations and consequent listing of koala as a species threatened in the north, provide an opportunity for increased funding to potentially outstrip VIC's massive expenditure.

This is not to say that expenditure in the north hasn't already been very wasteful in its own right. For example, in New South Wales there have been numerous state-wide and regional postal or internet surveys which have provided virtually no useful data about koalas in forests. In addition, there have been very many labour-intensive faecal pellet surveys in minute areas of forest, providing very scant information about trees that a few unidentified koalas may have occupied. These uninformative data have been analysed in great detail by well-paid scientists, leading to government decisions to quarantine sustainable natural resources, and consequent loss of employment, as well as various subsidies to maintain smaller, less efficient and unsustainable, natural resource-based industries.

OEH apparently overlooked the data from our radio-tracking studies at Eden, and incorrectly reported that there is a lack of knowledge about disease and genetics. Some *highlights* of their new Koala Strategy are about throwing more money at studies of genetics and chlamydia, not to mention *citizen science surveys* and *an app to collect information about koalas*. Dr. Lunney, formerly of OEH, now an Independent Expert, gave some interesting testimony about *citizen science* to the NSW Koala Inquiry: *"you can use a lot of techniques* [for koalas] *that are not available for cryptic animals through citizen science"*.[2] A decade earlier, he was the lead author of a scientific paper about mail-out surveys (now 'citizen science') of koalas. It stated that: *"This cryptic animal ... can be hard to detect"*.[3] Obviously, they're a lot more visible now than they were before, but Lunney's affirmed testimony to the Inquiry was that they're *"declining at different rates in different locations"*.[2]

Much real field data, collected from forests at considerable expense, isn't being used to advance koala management and conservation. For example, there is unequivocal evidence from NSW north coast that koalas were formerly associated with dense regrowth from intensive timber harvesting[4], but have since increased throughout declining forests. They now occur at more than 64% of survey sites independently of any harvesting history.[5] Nevertheless, more money ($300,000) is being thrown at research into impacts of regeneration harvesting on koalas and their habitat.

This research is overseen by an expert panel of three, assembled to deliver a *"robust and scientifically credible research program"*. The panel includes Dr Whisson and Mr Melzer of the ubiquitous seventeen and a half, and also of the numerically gifted fifteen. Two of three projects will investigate timber harvest impacts on koala nutrition[6], even though it is clear that harvesting no longer has any impact because the overwhelming influence is continuous cycling of new foliage in trees declining for want of mild fire.[7] (I presume the research will be replaced by post-megafire monitoring. See Postscript).

One project will be led by Dr. Ben Moore, also of the gifted fifteen, who in 2015 was apparently unable to recognise eucalypt decline. During a discussion about koala irruptions in *The Conversation*, I mentioned a multi-million dollar experiment in chronically declining red gum forest at his Western Sydney campus.[8] After my comment was seemingly censored without any *conversation*, Moore said this was a *"totally unrelated matter"* and he could disprove my *"impression"* (presumably that the trees were sick) gained from a *"brief visit"*, by using data from soils and foliage[xxviii].[9] I no longer bother with *The Conversation*.[xxix]

As a rough indication of the size of the salaries component of recent expenditure on koala research, I offer the following *back of the beer coaster* calculation: 18 experts X 25 years (the stated median time frame of their analyses) X $100K mean salary = $45 Million. NSW is committed to spend another $45 Million over three years on a Koala Strategy. This is on top of the cost of all the parliamentary and bureaucratic deliberations that paved the way for the Commonwealth listing and the State strategy.

[xxviii] I recommend that readers visit the EucFACE website to view, on the front page, the dense young, chronically declining forest with discoloured epicormic crowns, and decide for themselves: https://www.westernsydney.edu.au/hie/EucFACE

[xxix] In late 2019, *The Conversation* apparently announced that it would no longer allow debate about causes of climate change. *The Australian* Environment Editor, Graham Lloyd, rightly criticised this as *"consensus enforcement"*. Ironically, Lloyd is seemingly 'enforcing the consensus' on koalas that denies the first century of our European history (Introduction).

For example, NSW commissioned an *independent review* by the *Chief Scientist and Engineer*, into the 'decline' of koala populations in key areas of the State. I've no idea how much it cost but it doesn't seem to have been good value for money. It was largely informed by a report from Dr. Martin Predavec of OEH, on *NSW koala population case studies*.[10] Interestingly, neither the Office of the Chief Scientist, nor OEH took ownership of the *case studies*. They were published with the Chief Scientist's review as a "*Document prepared by Martin Predavec*". Perhaps this is a sign of independence.

In any case, Predavec regurgitated a lot of incorrect material published by OEH. For example, he reported:

> *A drastic long-term decline of koalas at Eden.*
> *A decrease in koalas after European settlement at Campbelltown,*
> *A stable to slowly declining population at Coffs Harbour.*
> *That there is no long-term ecological history for Pilliga-Liverpool Plains.*
> *And, that koalas survived the Millennium Drought in the* "*moister areas*" *of the Pilliga.*

Predavec was one of the researchers who found that koalas persisted in the hot and dry areas of the western Pilliga. Despite much seeming obfuscation in their report, their statistical analysis revealed that there was no significant association of koala persistence with moister areas near drainage lines.[11]

A Koala Advisory Committee was convened to assist the Chief Scientist. Associate Professor Johnathon Rhodes, from the gifted fifteen, was one of two *Independent Researchers*. He was a co-author with those who incorrectly reported the extinction of koalas at Eden for a second time[12], and was also amongst the group promoting email surveys as an efficient way to find koalas in north coast forests.[13] Rhodes, based on the Koala Coast, is an associate editor of *Journal of Applied Ecology*, but not the one who suggested I apparently "*misrepresented*" literature about the Koala Coast (she's from the UK). Dr. Brad Law of DPI was an *Agency Representative*. Using an effective technique, he found lots of koalas in north coast forests, and established that timber harvest has no influence on their numbers or distribution.[5] Law has since been funded to research impacts of timber harvesting on north coast koalas.

The Chief Scientist's report was published in December 2016[14], and submissions were invited to *NSW Koala Strategy*, closing 3rd March 2017. My submission stated that:

> *There is a fatal flaw in this process of developing a "strategy to stabilise and then start to increase koala numbers". There are many more koalas in New South Wales and Australia, over a much larger range, than there were at the time of European settlement. Where koalas are declining, they are declining from unnaturally high and unsustainable levels in declining forests and woodlands. A sensible strategy would be to restore healthy ecosystems with very few koalas, as existed when frequent mild burning by Aborigines maintained resilient ecosystems over about 40,000 years, including periods of extreme climate change ...*

> *NSW Koala Strategy must recognize that stable populations of koalas are virtually invisible, and that visible populations are unstable – a sign of ecological imbalance. The strategy should be to reinstate frequent mild burning, grazing or slashing to conserve healthy (and fire-safe) eucalypt ecosystems with very low, but sustainable, densities of koalas ...*

> *Please also note my concern that OEH is charged with assessing public feedback. This is clearly a case of setting the fox to mind the chooks.*

In their *Public engagement summary report*, OEH[15] stated that

> *The majority of submissions received supported the development of a whole-of-government koala strategy. Five submissions were critical of developing a strategy. These submissions expressed concerns about the data that will inform decision-making, and questioned the information underpinning the review.*

This suggests to me that five submissions were wrongly dismissed. Certainly, I argued that a strategy must be based on an understanding of ecological history. This was not critical of developing a strategy. However, the concerns about the data *"underpinning the review"* were apparently not addressed.

When my *Ecological history of the koala*[16] was provisionally accepted for publication by *Wildlife Research*, I contacted the office of Environment Minister, the Hon. Gabrielle Upton, and arranged a meeting with one of her advisors. In July 2017, I travelled to Sydney for the meeting and provided a copy of my book *Firestick Ecology*[17] in addition to other material and information. At the conclusion of the meeting, I was told "*We'll be in touch*" and that's the last I ever heard.

After my *Review* was finally accepted by *Wildlife Research* in October, I contacted the Office of the Chief Scientist in November to advise her that she had seemingly been misled by OEH and academics. On 6th December 2017, I received the following response.

> *Dear Mr Jurskis*
>
> *Professor Mary O'Kane asked that I thank you for your email in relation to your recently published paper on the ecological history of the koala. Professor O'Kane has forwarded the link to your paper to the NSW Office of Environment & Heritage for their consideration as they are developing the whole-of-government NSW Koala Strategy.*
>
> *Kind regards,*
>
> *Rebecca Radford*

I repeated my offer to brief Professor O'Kane on the facts about koalas. Sometime later, having received no further communication, I phoned her office to seek a meeting. I was informed that there was no reason to meet, as she would soon no longer be the Chief Scientist.

In February 2018, NSW announced four million dollars funding for new research led by Professor Ross Bradstock at Wollongong University. He succeeded Professor Whelan who sat on the Bushfires Inquiry that recommended research before land management.[17] Three of the four key foci of the research are:

> *impacts and management of hazard reduction burns*
> *drivers of bushfire frequency and severity*
> *impacts on the environment and endangered plants and animals*[18]

Bradstock helped to build a model which supposedly shows that prescribed burning mostly doesn't work for *biogeographical* reasons, and that it actually promotes wildfires in the region around Eden.[19]

In March 2018, 60 homes were destroyed by wildfire at Tathra (near Eden) and koalas were possibly killed in a nearby Flora Reserve dedicated to their protection. Bradstock said that lack of burning wasn't a factor in the disaster. The Rural Fire Service backed him, reporting that 93 hazard reduction "*activities*" were carried out in the previous 11 years covering 517 hectares.[20] That's a piddling average of 6 hectares per activity and 8 activities per year totalling 49 hectares.

Bradstock said broadscale burning is ineffective, whilst narrow breaks around houses can create "*defensible space*". But he admitted that houses at Tathra were ignited by long distance ember storms driven by high winds.[20] The fire jumped the Bega River and much of Tathra because it was fed by embers from heavy elevated fuels in long unburnt bush far away.

The Working Plan for the new koala reserves says:

> *Fire is a major threat to koalas. We will help protect them from fire by applying low intensity burns in small patches in appropriate locations surrounding identified areas of koala activity to provide low-fuel buffers against wildfire.*[21]

This is half a century after Athol Hodgson described the real-world situation, where such a strategy cannot possibly protect either koalas or houses during severe weather.[22]

In May 2018, NSW Koala Strategy was announced. The Acting Chief Scientist heads up an Advisory Panel of four, including Associate Professor Johnathon Rhodes. Early in June, at a public meeting in Eden, NSW Natural Resources Commission made some statements about the strategy that shocked me. I challenged them and received what I regarded as unsatisfactory responses. The following day I emailed the Commission. Here is an extract:

> **Re: Koala prescriptions, wood supply, scientific data and NSW Koala Strategy.**
>
> *At the public meeting about the IFOA in Eden yesterday I learnt of your report ... and your plan to carry out research about*

impacts of intensive harvesting on koalas. I'm disturbed by the suggestion that it is not possible to satisfy the dual objectives of timber supply and koala conservation ... the problem is not a lack of data, but [the way it is represented by] *experts.*

... the koala is inappropriately listed as a vulnerable species in NSW under ... State and Commonwealth legislation. The Strategy of stabilising and increasing numbers is not only inappropriate, but unachievable. Reduced numbers are a precondition for stability and increased numbers are clearly shown by history to be unsustainable. This has been evident in Victoria for more than a century ...

I raised these issues with the office of the Minister for the Environment and I have had no response. I will therefore not raise the issue separately with OEH through the feedback system for IFOAs.[xxx]

I attached eight scientific papers supporting my case.

I met with Dr. John Keniry AM, Commissioner, and Mr. Jeffrey Bell, Principal Advisor, of NRC on 3rd July. Mr. Bell indicated that he was involved in discussions with Dr. Brad Law about koala research. On 4th July I emailed them with five additional scientific papers. I ended my message as follows: "*John, I believe you've given me a fair hearing but no prospects for resolution of the issues. I believe that you are in a unique position giving you the opportunity to put the facts before the Premier.*[xxxi] *I request that you do so.*"

I received no further communication from NRC. On 31st October, a paper by Law and colleagues was published[5], stating that north coast koalas were **not** "*influenced by timber harvesting intensity, time since harvesting or local landscape extent of harvesting or old growth ... Retention forestry*[xxxii] *has a significant role to play in mitigating harvesting impacts ... but localised studies are needed to optimise prescriptions for koalas*".

I'm apparently rather lonely in finding a seeming contradiction

---

[xxx] Integrated Forestry Operations Approvals: more accurately a hotchpotch of prohibitions

[xxxi] The NRC now reports to the Minister for Planning

[xxxii] *Retention forestry* retains trees and/or intact forest patches at the time of harvest with the aim of conserving forest biodiversity

within this statement. On 6th November, I emailed NRC about Law's paper and related matters:

> *It calls for more research to supposedly optimise prescriptions intended to conserve koalas in multiple use forests and I suspect that it aims to justify the research project that you foreshadowed* [at the Eden meeting] *in June.*
>
> *I attach herewith a brief critique of the paper by Law and colleagues. Please provide details of the new koala research project as previously requested, and how it relates to existing scientific knowledge.*
>
> *Also, I recently heard that there have been some discussions between NRC, Forestry Corporation and others regarding chronic eucalypt decline. As the leading and most widely published authority on this problem in Australia, I offer you my assistance in developing a strategy to deal with it.*

So-called *BMAD* has been identified as a threat to koala habitat. It is but one limited facet of chronic eucalypt decline in the absence of mild fire. After decades of spending millions of dollars on researching bellbirds and psyllids, NSW recently spent $100,000 on a literature review of *BMAD*, which incorrectly concluded that bellbirds "*facilitate sustained psyllid infestations that lead to dieback*".[xxxiii] This *independent* review[24] was governed by a committee that included Dr. Christine Stone —possibly the foremost proponent of the flawed hypothesis that bellbirds cause chronic eucalypt decline. The co-author of the *independent* review, Dr. Angus Carnegie, is on her staff.

So-called *Grey Box Psyllid Dieback* near Sydney is another tiny facet of chronic eucalypt decline in the absence of mild burning, and also an identified threat to koala habitat. In this case, psyllids supposedly kill trees without assistance from bellbirds. NSW funded research on this problem to the tune of $415,000.[25] Koala expert Dr. Ben Moore, who was seemingly unable to recognise

---

[xxxiii] This has supposedly been demonstrated in retrospective studies by Dr. Christine Stone, which seemingly dismiss real-world, real-time observations that bellbirds increase in response to irruptions of psyllids in declining forests. Forests and Wood Products Australia funded some other academics to promote a scheme, based on the disproven *BMAD* hypothesis, to tap into a GreenHouseGas Emissions Reduction Fund.[23]

chronic eucalypt decline on his campus in Western Sydney, was involved in this research. Psyllids are but one of a wide range of arbivores, including koalas, that can temporarily benefit from forest decline.

On 7th November, I received a prompt, if rather uninformative, response to my email, from NRC:

> *Apologies we did not respond to you earlier following that meeting.*
> *We are aware of the research you've highlighted and will explore deeper the contradictions you've pointed out and will share with the team as we consider our own research.*
> *To give you a quick update on our koala research project:*
> *As part of the NSW Koala strategy, the Commission will lead new independent research on how koalas respond to native forest regeneration harvesting (also known as intensive harvesting) in North Coast state forests ...*
> *In regards to forest dieback we are doing some further homework on this issue. We have read your publications on dieback that you have previously shared – thank you. At this stage, we are not initiating a project on dieback, rather simply gathering more knowledge.*

Here are the highlights of the $45 million koala strategy as extolled by OEH[26]:

Koala Strategy highlights

Create over 24,000 hectares of new koala reserves and parks.
Fix priority road-kill hotspots across NSW.
Deliver a network of koala hospitals.
Create a new single wildlife rescue call number.
Develop a statewide koala habitat information base.
Conduct a citizen science survey to improve koala knowledge.
Designate the Australian Museum as the official biobank for koala genetic material.
Pilot an app to collect information about koalas.
Increase wildlife care training for veterinarians and veterinary nurses.
Relocate koalas to unoccupied koala habitat.
Research to significantly reduce incidence of chlamydia.
Deliver priority research under a research plan informed by a research symposium.
Monitor koala populations and their habitat through a statewide, cross-tenure koala monitoring program.

I was pleasantly surprised at the green reaction to the koala strategy. In a most uncharacteristic understatement, WWF announced:

NSW Koala Strategy: "ineffective, inadequate and expensive".

But they quickly reverted to seeming hyperbole and science fiction: *"The Strategy will not prevent the projected extinction of koalas, which WWF has found could be as early as 2050."*[27] This statement was picked up by the ALP candidate for Coffs Harbour in March 2019: *"If we don't do something by 2050 koalas are going to be extinct".*

*Australian Associated Press Fact-Check*ed the candidate's statement and found it to be mostly true, even though they said NSW Department of Primary Industries had found 10 times more koalas in the northeast region than previously thought.[xxxiv] AAP referred to the outlandish Senate report that there were up to ten million koalas throughout eastern Australia before whitefellas arrived, and relied on straight line extrapolations of crashes in unsustainably dense populations during the Millennium Drought.[28,29] At the same time *Fact-Check* wrongly 'convicted' the Nationals candidate, now member for Coffs Harbour, Mr. Gurmesh Singh, of falsely stating that koala numbers are far higher than in the past.

So much for: *"Restoring confidence in public statements by independently testing and verifying the facts".* The non-factual *Fact-Check* was 'picked up' by at least 44 newspapers in all States/Territories and *SBS* television. I asked AAP to *Fact-Check* the Senate report of millions of koalas when whitefellas arrived. They asked me for information from Bill Phillips' book for future reference. In May 2019, I asked AAP to check WWF's claim that *"Just 230 years ago, many millions of koalas roamed*

[xxxiv] In July 2018, DPI reported on their website: *"A major new study ... has found evidence for up to 10 times the rate of koala occupancy in NSW's north-east forests than previously estimated".* Three months later, their article in a scientific journal stated that koala occupancy *"was at least five times more than expected".* In March 2019, *Factcheck* reported: *"It* [the study] *found there were 10 times the number of koalas".*

the great forests and bushland of eastern Australia". Mr. James Lane of *Fact-Check*, thrice replied to my emails, that *we'll have a look*, or words to that effect, but nothing happened.

On 22nd September 2019, I supplied six scientific papers and requested a correction of the statement by *Fact-Check* that "*There was only one study ... which found any evidence of an increase* [in koalas]". I pointed out that *Fact-Check*'s conclusion, that Mr. Singh's statement was mostly false, was wrong. Four days later, the newly appointed Editor, Peter Trute, replied that "*I'll review your material and respond.*" AAP states that:

> *Inaccuracies or suspected inaccuracies that affect the integrity of stories published by* **AAP Fact-Check** *will be dealt with promptly. An initial response can be expected within one business day, but more usually within an hour of a problem coming to our attention. When we acknowledge an inaccuracy, a correction will be urgently issued.*

On 22nd November, after seven inconsequential emails and a phone call from Mr Trute, I lodged a complaint with AAP's *Standards Committee* referring to inaccurate statements, incorrect conclusions, inadequate responses and seeming breaches of their code of conduct by AAP FactCheck. I have received no response. FactCheck's article on koalas was altered to remove the incorrect statement, but the incorrect conclusion remains uncorrected because there is supposedly a "*consensus that koala numbers are declining*".

On 1st October 2019, I had taken a few hours off from the final edit of my manuscript to attend a 'public engagement' by NRC in Eden. They were promoting a nine million dollar forest monitoring and improvement scheme to check management performance and outcomes against the rules, based on the wilderness myth, that are causing all our environmental problems.

One of their four scientific advisers is Associate Professor Philip Gibbons, who, with colleagues from the Fenner School at ANU, published a paper that seems to promote dense, unmanaged, chronically declining, scrub-infested forests with three-dimensionally continuous fuels including lots of dead wood, as benchmarks for healthy ecosystems.[30] Unnaturally high loads of dead wood[31] are desired as a 'positive outcome' under the monitoring scheme. Another adviser is Professor Patrick Baker who co-authored an article[32] which seemed to refer to extensive clearing of river red gum forests that never existed and loss of fallen timber that wasn't there.[33] He was also one of more than 200 authors who apparently contributed to a four page article published in *Nature* about averting collapse of biodiversity.[34]

On 18th October I received NRC's draft monitoring program "*For public review*". The NRC package includes a million dollars directed to monitoring forest health or so-called die-back[xxxv] in relation to timber harvesting rules[35] which are irrelevant to forest health. Seemingly, this is different to the program they were "*not initiating*" 11 months earlier when I offered to assist their investigations of chronic eucalypt decline. I'm constantly impressed by the ability of bureaucrats to politely nod at verbal submissions and politely acknowledge email submissions, then proceed with their apparently pre-ordained plans. I'm sure they enjoy getting out of the city for their *public engagements*, but it costs a lot of money and doesn't seem to satisfy anybody's desire to contribute to real improvements in ecosystem management.

The NRC's Forest Monitoring and Improvement Scheme, like the NSW Koala Strategy, is bureaucracy gone mad. You don't even have to walk outside, to see the deplorable state of forests across all tenures. You need only turn on the television. It doesn't matter what show you watch, if there is bush in the background, you'll see either dying trees and booming scrub, or dying trees and flaming scrub. Nevertheless, NRC Assistant Commissioner Peter Cochrane, Professor Baker and others visited the Eden region on 26th November to have a look at the problem. At the end of the day, Baker thanked me for my 'views', whereas

---

[xxxv] Dieback can be a natural response to acute stress such as drought. Drought scorch was apparent in stunted trees on rocky ridgetops north of Bega in 2006 and again in September 2019. They recovered full, healthy mature crowns between the two events. Meanwhile, extensive chronic decline and mortality of tall trees on the higher quality midslope and gully sites in these unlogged National Parks continued unabated.

another scientific adviser, Dr. Peter Hairsine, thanked me for my information and said that he'd learnt a great deal.

Professor Baker was apparently of the opinion that we couldn't afford to restore a safe and healthy landscape using mild fire even if we wanted to, but seemingly oblivious to the bitter irony of spending nine million dollars developing a new monitoring scheme. At this stage, we don't need more monitoring, we need active adaptive management.

At NSW Koala Inquiry, traditional burning expert Victor Steffensen described the problem of accelerated scrub invasion after megafires[36]:

> *the invasive wattles, tea-trees and other plants that are totally flammable get up over six-foot high ... so thick that it starts to lose the value and identity of those ecosystems.*
>
> *We need recovery teams out there right now ... in the next season burning leaf litter to breakdown and kill the young invasive flammable ones and start ... to bring up the right plants and the right grasses to come back in that country that is going to be lower, healthy with more food sources and diversity.*

A week later, with the megafires still uncontained, NRC announced a *Foundational Project Supporting post-fire ecological resilience and recovery planning in NSW forests*. They are going to use satellite imagery at regular intervals to monitor the development of invasive scrub as a measure of *"post-fire ecological recovery"*![37]

Notes

1   Menkhorst 2008
2   Lunney 2019 pp. 11, 16.
3   Lunney *et al.* 2009
4   Kavanagh *et al.* 1995
5   Law *et al.* 2018
6   NRC 2019a
7   Jurskis *et al.* 2011
8   University of Western Sydney 2019
9   Moore and Whisson 2015

10 Predavec 2016

11 Lunney *et al.* 2017b p. 284

12 Lunney *et al.* 2014

13 Brown *et al.* 2018

14 O'Kane 2016

15 OEH 2018a

16 Jurskis 2017a

17 Jurskis 2015

18 NSW Government 2018

19 Price *et al.* 2015 Figure 3

20 Hannam 2018

21 Forestry Corporation and OEH 2017

22 Hodgson 1968

23 Smith and Ximenes 2019 p. 83

24 Silver and Carnegie 2017

25 University of Western Sydney 2013

26 OEH 2018b

27 WWF 2018a

28 Evans *et al.* 2019

29 WWF 2018b

30 Jurskis 2015 p. 9

31 Jurskis 2011a

32 MacNally *et al.* 2011

33 Jurskis 2015 Ch. 11

34 Laurance *et al.* 2012

35 NRC 2019b

36 Steffensen 2019 p. 27

37 NRC 2019c

7

DÉJÀ VU

State forest services were established in the early 20th Century by foresters trained in Europe and imbued with the principles of Colonial Forestry, especially fire suppression.[1] Consequently, woody thickening and accumulation of three-dimensionally continuous fuels led to disastrous megafires as well as to chronic decline of eucalypt forests and outbreaks of arbivores.[2] In 1939, the Black Friday megafires killed 77 people, burnt two million hectares of Victoria and southeast New South Wales, and destroyed 69 sawmills.

Despite the extreme weather conditions, many fires in far East Gippsland at the same time caused little damage. Forests east of the Snowy River were mostly controlled by the Lands Department and burnt by graziers, keeping them open, healthy and safe.[2,3] John Mulligan was there. His family wasn't worried, even when his uncle's car repeatedly stopped because of vapour locks in the fuel lines with the extreme heat.[4] A map of the fires in Victoria shows an extreme contrast. A million hectares of unbroken fire extended from the Murray River north of Corryong and southwesterly along the Great Dividing Range to Melbourne. The 14 'large' fires mapped in far East Gippsland were miniscule in proportion.[5]

In the absence of mild burning, highland forests of southeastern Australia were devastated by plagues of phasmids from the 1940s to the early 1960s.[6] Thousands of hectares of hydroelectric catchments were aerially sprayed with dangerous insecticides in diesel fuel to control the stick insects.[7,8] Psyllids plagued forests in coastal New South Wales and bellbirds responded by irrupting and extending their range.[2,8,9] At the same time, koalas, thought to have become extinct in NSW by the 1920s, began to reappear.[10]

Foresters belatedly realized the futility and destructiveness of attempted fire suppression. In 1951, The Hume-Snowy Bushfire Prevention Scheme was established to protect hydroelectric catchments, timber and pastures in New South Wales' Alps using prescribed burning.[11] In 1961, the Dwellingup Megafire burnt hundreds of thousands of hectares of forest and destroyed four towns in Western Australia. Trials of aerial ignition were initiated in 1965 to improve the extent and efficiency of prescribed burning. These trials extended to the Australian Alps and east coast hinterland by 1967/8.[12] An aerial burn saved Bega from wildfire during the following fire season[13] when over a million hectares were burnt, 14 people were killed, and more than 150 homes and buildings were lost in other parts of NSW.[14]

Forest health, structure and fire safety temporarily improved.[11,15,16,17] No significant occurrences of chronic eucalypt decline or pest outbreaks were reported in New South Wales' State Forests for the next quarter of a century.[15] In Western Australia, an outbreak of gum leaf skeletoniser across 90,000 hectares of southern jarrah forest in the 1980s had little or no impact on areas that had been deliberately burnt up to three years earlier. Burning didn't directly control the insects[18], rather it maintained resilience of trees.[16]

An unprecedented spike in charcoal deposition—a measure of burnt biomass—during 70,000 years had occurred after Europeans disrupted Aboriginal burning, followed by a pronounced decline after foresters reinstated mild burning in the late 20th Century.[19] Fifty years of data on the efficacy of broadscale prescribed burning in southwestern Australia showed a strong inverse correlation ($R^2 = 0.77$) between area subsequently burnt by wildfires compared to area of prescribed burning, provided that, on average, more than ~ 1at least 8-10% of the forests had been burnt preceding years. The relationship held, despite great variability in climate and in the area treated each year, through a period of warming and drying climate.[17,20,21,22]

Burning reduced the number and the extent of wildfires, especially megafires.[22] From 1962-1990, the mean annual area burnt by prescribed fire and wildfire was 12.5% and 0.3% respectively. From 1991-2012, the mean treated area fell to 6.6% and, despite superior detection and suppression capability, the area burnt by wildfire increased almost four-fold to 1.1%.[23] From 2011-2015, the annual area treated declined to ~ 3.5% whilst the area burnt by wildfire increased threefold to ~ 3.1%.[21]

Three percent of State Forest in New South Wales was treated annually by prescribed burning in the decade to 2003 and a slightly smaller area was burnt by wildfires. Burning occurred mainly in coastal areas where a substantially higher proportional area was burnt. During the same period, 0.4% of National Park was treated each year whilst twelve times the area (2.5 million hectares) was burnt by wildfires.[15] Between 1997 and 2006 an average of 0.4% of the Sydney Basin was treated by prescribed burning each year whilst 4.2% was burnt by wildfires.[24]

From about 1980, ecologists with no experience of mild burning had raised concerns that it would eliminate plants that are unable to resprout and animals that require dense understoreys or fallen timber for food or shelter. The silly idea that life histories of supposedly fire-sensitive plants, which had thrived during millennia of Aboriginal burning, should be used to determine intervals between prescribed fires was eagerly accepted. Many studies of fire regimes and life cycles of plants were published, and NSW NPWS eventually produced *Guidelines for Ecologically Sustainable Fire Management* that specify *"acceptable fire intervals"* for all types of vegetation in the State.

Prescribed burning was progressively reduced from the late 20th Century.[15,17,21,23] After the 1970s, 'strategic' burning with broader fire suppression was introduced to National Parks around Sydney. Biomass accumulated, biodiversity declined, health of some trees and shrubs declined, disease flourished and a vicious circle of high intensity fire was initiated.[25] Megafires have occurred in southern Australia at an average rate of once a year since the turn of the millennium.[2,14] Chronic eucalypt decline increased dramatically in the late 20th Century, and is now widespread along with irruptions of arbivores including psyllids, beetles, weevils, caterpillars, fungi, koalas, possums, mistletoes and parasitic shrubs and vines.[2,8,16]

"A Nation Charred" in 2003 learnt its lesson, that *"there has been grossly inadequate hazard reduction burning on public lands for far too long; local knowledge and experience is being ignored by an increasingly top heavy bureaucracy"*.[26] The bureaucracy in southeastern Australia seemingly boycotted the

Nairn Inquiry, but consulted behind closed doors with another headed by an emergency chief and two academics. This *COAG Inquiry* decided that the main problem in 2003 was *"prolonged drought ... above-average temperatures and a much higher incidence of lightning strikes"*. Their solution was *"Learning how to live with bushfire"*.[27] Since then, more than 200 people have been killed.

Almost 20% of coastal forests and woodlands in New South Wales were declining by 2010[28] and the proportion continues to increase rapidly, along with the range of forest types affected, whilst frequent mild burning disappears in accordance with the *Guidelines*. For example, despite the Millennium Drought in the first decade of this Century, spotted gum and blackbutt forests on well drained sites were not declining. Now all types of forest are chronically declining. By 2014, more than 50% of eucalypt ecosystems in Queensland's Wet Tropics World Heritage Area were affected by chronic decline due to lack of burning.[29] Things are just as bad in NSW, and worse in East Gippsland VIC where phytophthora seems to be running rampant again.

The situation is much worse now than it was 50 years ago, when foresters applied adaptive management before the term was coined. It is very difficult to find examples of well managed forests with healthy trees. In NSW, it is illegal, in practical terms, to manage forests sustainably using frequent mild fire. For example, health, safety and biodiversity can be maintained in eucalypt forests by mild burning every three to six years[30], whereas the NSW *Bush Fire Environmental Assessment Code* specifies minimum intervals of ten years between fires in dry shrubby forests and thirty years in moist shrubby forests[xxxvi].[31] The rules and procedures for burning in NSW now virtually ensure moderate to high intensity hazard **production** burns in most cases.

Even the lowest fire intensities achievable in heavy fuels can cause severe environmental damage. My extended family burnt some gum-applebox woodland in winter 2019 late in the evening in light drizzle. Any mature gum trees that we had not

---

[xxxvi] Virtually all eucalypt forests on public lands are shrub-invaded because of lack of mild burning and/or grazing. Moist, shrub invaded forests are wrongly classified as wet sclerophyll forests by NPWS and RFS.[32]

raked around were killed because the moderate intensity and long residence time of the fire in the accumulated litter killed the sapwood and epicormic buds at the base of the trees and on the exposed roots. By contrast, lignotuberous seedlings in grassy gaps with light fuels were killed back to the soil surface by the quickly burning low-intensity fire and soon resprouted.

In our public forests, large blocks are planned, from the office, for burning years later. Long lines of fire are lit around perimeters, attaining maximum rates of spread and intensities within minutes.[33] They are often lit from the bottoms of slopes and across the wind, just wherever the boundary track happens to be. Canopies are scorched, trees are burnt down and understories are thickened by dense germination and resprouting. These dangerous and destructive practices are self-fulfilling green academics' prophecies that burning is bad for the environment.

I'm sick of hearing that we can no longer apply mild fire because climate change is closing the window of opportunity. When I started as a forester on NSW north coast, burning was easy and safe and enjoyable. We didn't use written plans and rules and regulations and perimeter tracks and drip torches and fire engines. We used commonsense, matches and suitable weather conditions in a healthy and safe landscape. It is the development of 3D continuous fuels with lack of burning that is closing the window, not climate change. Dense scrubby forests won't burn under mild conditions, except in a drought. But they explode in severe conditions causing firestorms and ember showers that destroy lives and homes of people and animals, generating untold carbon emissions. The more mild fire we apply, the easier and safer and more environmentally friendly it gets. Foresters proved that fifty years ago, only forty thousand years after Aborigines established mild burning as the basis for their culture and economy.

Traditional knowledge and science inform us that the landscape should be gifted with fire progressively as fuels develop and cure, and the vegetation becomes receptive. Fire should be applied firstly in exposed areas, in spots that gradually coalesce whilst humidity increases as the sun goes down. Spots should be lit progressively into the wind.[12,33] Hilly country needs lighting from the top down, and fire should be extended to sheltered aspects and gullies as they warm and dry. Unfortunately, fire management is now regulated by emergency junkies who prefer hugely expensive and ineffective water bombing operations during disasters, rather than cheap, efficient and safe aerial delivery of sustaining fire to maintain healthy landscapes and prevent disasters.

Notes

1   Underwood 2013
2   Jurskis 2015
3   Attiwill *et al.* 2009
4   John Mulligan, East Gippsland Wildland Fire Taskforce, pers. comm.
5   Luke and McArthur 1978 p. 308, fig. 23.2
6   Campbell 1966
7   Campbell and Hadlington 1967
8   Jurskis and Turner 2002
9   Moore 1961
10 Anon. 1950
11 Jurskis *et al.* 2006
12 Underwood 2015
13 Cheney 2015
14 Adams and Attiwill 2011
15 Jurskis *et al.* 2003
16 Jurskis 2005
17 Sneeuwjagt 2008
18 Farr *et al.* 2004
19 Mooney *et al.* 2011
20 Adams and Attiwill 2011 Fig. 7.1
21 Burrows 2016b
22 Boer *et al.* 2009
23 Burrows and McCaw 2013
24 Penman *et al.* 2011
25 Jurskis and Underwood 2013
26 House of Representatives Select Committee 2003
27 Ellis, Kanowski and Whelan 2004
28 Jurskis and Walmsley 2011
29 Stanton *et al.* 2014
30 Jurskis 2011b
31 RFS 2006 p. 28
32 Jurskis 2015 Ch. 12
33 Jurskis 2015 p. 190

8

CRUELTY TO ANIMALS

Old Sheppie, he knew he was goin' to go
For he reached out and licked at my hand
Arthur Williams and Red Foley 1932

Greens make no bones about using the koala as an icon to prevent economic development of natural resources. They claim that its iconic status makes it useful to protect habitat for less charismatic species. That's ridiculous because conditions favouring irruptions of koalas make habitat unsuitable for the truly endangered fauna that are suffering as scrub proliferates with mismanagement of our landscape. Our major socio-ecological problems of megafires and species extinctions are consequences of excluding mild fire from 'protected' areas.[1] Any of the tightly regulated clearing that occurs in Australia pales into insignificance as a potential threat to wildlife.

Both animal welfare and environmental conservation could be addressed by sensible management, but it's not happening. WWF's blueprint for koala conservation is a *Koala Habitat Conservation Plan.*[2] Produced in collaboration with two animal welfare organisations (*Humane Society International* and *International Fund for Animal Welfare*), as well as four broader green groups, it is clearly focussed on land management, or more accurately, on non-management. On the other hand, *NSW Koala Strategy*[3] is a hotchpotch of animal welfare and land reservation programs. I suspect this may represent a ploy by people who perhaps have one foot in either camp—ENGO and government bureaucracy. The overt ENGO players can criticise the bureaucracy for not supporting politically difficult schemes such as creation of a *Great Koala National Park*[4], whilst knowing that their animal welfare constituency is assured of overt bureaucratic support.

In the early Nineteenth Century, when John Gould was worried that koalas would become extinct, he wasn't concerned about animal welfare. Gould shot koalas, and Aborigines hurled clubs to knock them out of trees for him.[5] Later, Arthur Ransome famously wrote of collecting fauna—*What's hit's history: what's missed's mystery.*[6] Gould was not only a collector, but also a precursor to the likes of Sir David Attenborough. However, video technology wasn't available then, and wild animals generally don't sit for artistic portraits.

In a recent tome about Gould's musings on endangered Australian fauna, Dr. Fred Ford made much of the fur trade.[7] However this didn't actually commence until long after Gould had returned to England and written his book. Gould was concerned because koalas were so rare. The koala fur industry was a pragmatic response to widespread irruptions of koalas that occurred much later. They were by then in plagues, and hunters certainly didn't regard shooting them as cruelty. Nevertheless, Ford seemed to disparage the *"mentality of the settlers"* and referred to *"frivolous shooting of Koalas for 'sport'."*

Dr. Ford wrote about a huge outcry against hunting in 1927. This was after dense southern populations had crashed during the Federation Drought. There was an open season in QLD because koalas were in plague proportions in the Central Districts, and common, i.e. visible, elsewhere (see Fig. 2 p. 75). They were still suffering malnutrition and disease.[8] The healthy, virtually invisible, but resilient, low-density populations in the south were not. They were thought to be mostly extinct.

In 1933, childrens' author Dorothy Wall had denounced the cruelty of hunting, but a passage from her book *Blinky Bill*[9], gives us a hint about the real *mentality* of shooters:

> *The koala family lived so happily; never thinking of harm, or anything that could happen to disturb their little home, as all they asked for were plenty of fresh gum-leaves and the warm sun. They had no idea such things as guns were in the world*

or that a human being had a heart so cruel that he would take a pleasure in seeing a poor little body riddled with bullets hanging helplessly from the tree-top. And they had no idea this same being would walk away, after shooting a bear, content to see him dead, no matter if he fell to the ground or not. That same being might just as well take his gun and shoot baby kookaburras, so helpless were they all and so trusting.

The thing is that baby kookaburras weren't diseased and starving to death. Blinky Bill's family was suffering. They didn't have *plenty of fresh gum leaves* because their declining trees were dying (e.g. see front and back cover). There will always be cruel individuals. However, the idea proposed by the likes of Dr. Ford and AKF, that there was a whole generation of greedy monsters heedless of cruelty to animals and now there are huge new industries in Australia intent on making money by means of environmental rape and pillage, is a particularly green ideology. Ironically, it underpins a multi-million dollar 'charitable' industry that is itself causing untold animal suffering.

As a supposedly *nasty, biased, anti-environmentalist fanatic* in *fallacious denial*, and *a forester who hates conservationists*, I can only say in my own defence that I am a fervent conservationist and lover of animals both wild and domestic. I became a forester because I loved the bush as it was when it was managed properly. Now I want to restore it. Green ideology has wrought environmental devastation and extreme cruelty to animals. I want to make the bush beautiful and healthy and safe again, even if that means that koalas are scarce, healthy, safe and invisible.

Modern experts who are using injections rather than firearms to put down starving koalas seem to be regarded as morally superior to shooters who were using a humane method (remember Old Shep?) and also harvesting a natural resource. In my view, the translocation programs are immoral. They have condemned tens of thousands of koalas to either a lingering death by starvation and/or disease or a violent confrontation with a predator or a motor vehicle.

The non-management of our public forests is even worse,

because more koalas are affected. For example, in The Pilliga alone, more than 80% (12,000) of an estimated 15,000 koalas perished during the Millennium Drought. The estimated 13,000 koalas in Gunnedah Shire surely suffered a similar disaster.[10] Even if only half of them died, that's 7,000. More than 20,000 koalas undoubtedly perished in the Pilliga – Liverpool plains region during a single drought. Further to the northeast, thousands of koalas are being incinerated in spring 2019 as fires rage through heavy fuels in neglected forests.

In 2015, Sydney's Koala Park was prosecuted by the Royal Society for Prevention of Cruelty to Animals and fined $75,000 for not properly looking after five koalas[11] (average $15K per animal). If all was fair, NPWS should cop a fine of $180 million, just for neglecting proper management of the Pilliga. Instead, they have been given $20 million to lock up more declining forest and cause more needless animal suffering.[3] NSW Koala Strategy is nothing short of stupidity. It aims to increase a problem and treat the symptoms. Certainly, there should be facilities to euthenase or rehabilitate sick or injured koalas, but why then send them back to war?

The pragmatic, scientific, economic and humane solution to koala conservation and welfare is to restore a healthy landscape and simultaneously reduce dense populations using ethical and effective means. Managers of eucalypt plantations are free to control irruptions of native insects or fungi by using pesticides. Koalas present much more complex socio-ecological challenges.

A short-term pragmatic solution would be to dampen irruptions by 'turning off' juvenile koalas for export to zoos around the world. For example, graziers routinely balance pasture production against breeding rates and sales of livestock. The supply of juvenile koalas might soon outstrip demand from institutions with suitable facilities and resources to sustain them, but new facilities would undoubtedly be established in response to a supply becoming available.

I know of one overseas park featuring Australian wildlife that has been unable to source koalas since their last animal died at an advanced age in 2016.[12] This park apparently has the necessary federal approvals to import koalas. I had discussions with the relevant diplomatic mission in Canberra, and attempted to establish contact between the theme park manager and a plantation manager in the Green Triangle who has operational difficulties with koalas in the blue gum plantations:

> They are a pest in the Eucalyptus globulus plantations in the Green Triangle. There were a few native koalas in the small areas of native forest scattered through the GT, but with the establishment of 180,000 ha of bluegum plantations, their population has exploded.[13]

When mature plantations are clearfelled, nine trees are left around each resident koala[14] until the koala strips them bare and moves on, presumably to some other habitat that is already occupied. Rather than fighting for a pragmatic solution to enhance animal welfare as well as timber production, the plantation manager responded: *"Our Government would never allow us to export wild koalas"*.[13]

This begs a question of definition of wild animals and their natural habitat. It also seems to confirm that animal welfare is not always an important consideration in politics. Nevertheless, research could be carried out in blue gum plantations to try and identify suitable regimes to manage soil conditions and tree spacings that would support maximum growth of trees without initiating unsustainable irruptions of koalas. Healthy, live koalas could be a valuable export commodity. The cost of such research would be a drop in the bucket, and the potential animal welfare and economic benefits great.

Frequent mild burning and/or grazing should be reintroduced into native forests and woodlands to restore ecosystem health and sustain healthy, very low-density populations of koalas. This would also address the immediate animal-welfare issue of injury or death by wildfires that is blindingly obvious as countless koalas are incinerated on NSW' north coast and the Koala

Coast hinterland in spring/summer 2019.[xxxvii] In the meantime, the issues of starvation and disease should be addressed by euthanasia of terminally ill koalas and export of young, as well as rehabilitated koalas, to zoological parks. Higher densities of koalas could be maintained in intensively managed regrowth forests, also by restoring forest health and safety with frequent mild burning.

More natural soil conditions and nutrient cycling processes, supporting healthy trees and sustainable densities of koalas, might be restored in improved pastures by applying specially tailored soil amendments and fertilizers, and reinstating native grasses and fire regimes. Landowners should be made aware of this potential option.

Unfortunately, in our crazy modern world, simple pragmatic solutions to perceived problems seemingly can't win votes. Governments need to be seen as bleeding hearts pumping billions of dollars into existential crises.

Notes

1 Jurskis 2015

2 WWF 2019

3 OEH 2018b

4 NPA 2019

5 Gould 1863

6 Ransome 1947

7 Ford 2014

8 Gordon and Hrdina 2005, Tables 6, 7; Figure 3

9 Wall 1933

10 Predavec 2016

11 Roberts 2016

12 G. Zuckermann pers. comm. 2018

13 email communications from a blue gum plantation manager

14 DELWP 2018

15 Morton 2019

16 Dye 20

[xxxvii] As well as destroying 44 homes and claiming 2 lives[15], the Busbys Flat fire engulfed *"one of the most important koala colonies on the North Coast"*, according to the North East Forest Alliance.[16]

9

THE LAST RESORT

The truth will set you free
Jesus Christ

But first it will piss you off
Gloria Steinem

In the decade after I graduated as a forester, ridiculous hypotheses and prescriptions dreamt up by city-based academics and bureaucrats with no practical knowledge or experience supplanted traditional knowledge, history, science and on-ground experience as the basis for land management. Then NSW passed the *Wilderness Act*, enshrining this mind-blowing transformation in legislation and bureaucracy!

Back then, I was optimistic that winding back sustainable industries which were using renewable natural resources produced by solar energy, employing people in rural areas, maintaining healthy and safe landscapes and locking up carbon in aesthetically pleasing structures, would eventually lead to a paradigm shift when we all had *the arse out of our trousers*.

Then we got free trade, the mining boom and urban explosion based on the immigration Ponzi scheme.[1] Now we import goods and materials unsustainably manufactured or extracted by slave labour in developing countries, and maintain our economic growth by immigration of skilled workers and consumers. So we still haven't worn out our proverbial trousers, but by 2018 we'd had nine quarters of negative per capita growth in our record 27 year run of economic growth.[1]

During the same period we've incorporated *Terra Nullius* or the wilderness myth into our National Forest Policy Statement. Urban explosion has ensured that government policy is unduly influenced by voters who have no connection with the bush, but a voracious appetite for green propaganda. Consequently we've experienced unprecedented environmental degradation, loss of biodiversity, loss of human life and socioeconomic destruction as a result of chronic eucalypt decline, scrub invasion and megafires, right across Australia.

Notably, this is happening in iconic reserves such as Kosciuszko National Park and World Heritage Areas including the Blue Mountains, the Gondwana Rainforests[2,3] and the Wet Tropics.[4] But, whatever the land tenure, you can't go anywhere or even turn the telly on without seeing sick and dying forests, booming scrub and, all too often, towering infernos. Widespread irruptions and declines of koalas are but one symptom of this environmental malaise, and they're being cynically used to deliver more of the same. The child oracles and climate warriors should be campaigning for mild burning as a fairdinkum *extinction rebellion* and a negative-cost means of reducing carbon emissions.

Having exhausted opportunities amongst academia, the media, the bureaucracy and ENGOs, to challenge the great koala scam, I made a submission to NSW Independent Commission Against Corruption on 9th December 2018. On 7th March 2019, I was advised by Assessment Officer, Ms. Alexandra Allsopp that:

> *The Commission will not be investigating your allegations ...*
> *... Overall, there is **limited** [my emphasis] objective information before the Commission to indicate that [any organisation or person] has engaged in corrupt conduct.*

Accordingly, on 24th March 2019, I made a new, very short submission to ICAC with objective information (data published by government agencies) that I had thoughtlessly neglected to supply in my previous submission. On 10th May and 10th September, I provided additional information. On 12th December I received a response from Ms. Allsopp, but this time it was signed by CEO, Mr. Philip Reed:

> *The further information you provided is substantially similar to the information you previously provided the Commission, about which we determined not to take any further action.*
>
> *Therefore, the Commission's decision not to investigate this matter stands. As a result, the matter is now closed.*
>
> *We will consider any further information you provide in writing. However, unless in the Commission's view it differs substantially from that already provided, we will not contact you again.*

I reckon that's a pretty clever way of saying we'll have no further correspondence unless it relates to a completely different matter.

I made a submission to the Legislative Council Inquiry into *Koala Populations and Habitat in New South Wales* on 23rd July and to the Senate Inquiry into *Australia's Faunal Extinction Crisis* on 27th July 2019. These submissions are on the web. I gave evidence to the Koala Inquiry on 9th December.

I made a submission on 11th December 2019, to the House of Representatives committee on Environment and Energy Inquiry into *the effects of land management on bushfires and consequent risks to our socioeconomic and natural environment* (my paraphrasing) This is also on the web. Since then, the megafires have escalated into gigafires and there have been various vague announcements about other inquiries.

While-ever our leaders continue to take advice from green academics and bureaucrats, emergency services generalissimos and misguided children, instead of people who know and love the land, our future will get progressively sadder and badder.

Notes

1   Barbones 2018
2   Jurskis 2015 p. 322
3   Horton 2012
4   Stanton *et al.* 2014

Postscript

Late in November 2019, I saw a koala crossing the Princes Highway south of Eden, where 'experts' claim they're extinct. Koalas were actually irrupting in chronically declining, scrub-infested forest either side of the Victorian border (Chapter 5). On 9th December, I tendered photos at NSW Koala Inquiry to illustrate the healthy koala, the declining trees and the *"three-dimensionally continuous fuel"* that can feed firestorms and megafires. Later that day, Mr. Oliver Costello of Firesticks Alliance Indigenous Corporation tabled a letter countersigned by officials of various green, animal welfare and indigenous groups, calling on the Committee of Inquiry to urge the Government to impose a moratorium on logging of koala habitat, in response to the megafires.

On 20th December, the NSW Planning Minister made *State Environmental Planning Policy (Koala Habitat Protection) 2019.* It *"aims to ... reverse the current trend of koala population decline"* by curtailing existing uses or new developments on private lands. *"This Policy* [apparently formulated by green bureaucrats] *commences on 1 March 2020 and is required to be published on the NSW legislation website."* To me, it seems not to fit the Cambridge Dictionary definition of legislation—*"laws suggested by a government and made official by a parliament"*. For example, the NSW Inquiry into koalas isn't due to report to Parliament until 15th June 2020. It seems that neither the great multitude of affected landholders, nor their elected representatives, have had any input or influence.

On 14th January 2020, *The Sydney Morning Herald* carried a front page headline—Koalas are barely clinging on. Under a cute picture of a joey clinging to the bottom side of a small branch, we were informed that *"Koalas could soon be listed as endangered in parts of Australia after large-scale habitat loss in the bushfires"*.

On 30th January, NSW Premier Gladys Berejiklian announced an independent inquiry into the catastrophic bushfires. It is to be conducted by a former deputy police commissioner, and former Chief Scientist, Professor Mary O'Kane. O'Kane headed the *"independent"* review which seemed to have adopted the incorrect conclusions of green academics and bureaucrats, that koalas were generally declining in NSW (Chapter 6). This review apparently led to the new *SEPP 2019* on 'protecting' koala habitat.

During late December/early January, vast areas of forests and very many koalas in East Gippsland VIC/Far South Coast NSW were incinerated by megafires, along with a number of small towns. The Princes Highway (Australia's Highway 1) in this area was finally reopened to through traffic in early February after extensive clearing of burnt-out trees along the roadway. I re-photographed the site where I saw the koala crossing the highway, and on 20th February 2020, offered to table at the Koala Inquiry, before and after photos of this site. As this book goes to press I have received no response from the secretariat or the Chairperson.

My photos, though technically poor, graphically illustrate the process of forest decline in the absence of mild fire; invasion of scrub, irruption of koalas, development of three-dimensionally continuous fuels; consequent explosive understorey and crown fire; and subsequent resprouting of an abundance of soft, juicy and nutritious eucalypt foliage. History indicates that dense forest, scrub, koalas and explosive fuels will 'recover' quickly. Healthy and safe landscapes will certainly not, unless we reinstate mild fire.

ACKNOWLEDGEMENTS

Friends and colleagues from NSW Forestry Commission and the timber industry, as well as other fairdinkum conservationists, too many to name, did great work over several years, to resolve the mystery of invisible koalas at Eden. I thank them all.

Colleagues and friends from across the political divide encouraged me, either to be more politically correct or potentially defamatory, especially Justin Black and John Turner. I hope that I have achieved the *Golden Mean* by offending both sides.

Neil Burrows, Phil Cheney and Roger Underwood have challenged my views, filled the many gaps in my knowledge and brought me to an holistic view of fire ecology.

David Packham is a bastion of science, and constantly reminds us of the fundamental truth that fire intensity is governed by fuel, not climate. David explains that, in the fuels which develop in forests deprived of frequent mild burning, rate of spread is proportional to the weight of fuel. Thus fire intensity is proportional to the weight of fuel multiplied by the weight of fuel. Byram's equation for fire intensity[1]: $I = Hwr$[xxxviii] becomes a quadratic equation, wherein doubling the fuel causes a fourfold increase in fire intensity.

Greg Gordon stands out as a genuine koala expert with an open mind and an appreciation of history. He has tried to help in my battle against groupthink.

Peter Rutherford has been a library of information and a warrior against the wilderness cult.

[xxxviii] I is fire intensity in kW/m; H is the heat yield in kJ/kg of fuel; w is the weight of fuel consumed in kg/m^2; r is the rate of spread in m/sec.[1]

My beloved Gwenny has been unbelievably tolerant, and my family extremely supportive, over the years I've been neglecting domestic affairs whilst indulging in a seemingly quixotic campaign to restore a beautiful, healthy and safe landscape.

Anthony Cappello stands out as a publisher with the courage to challenge unscientific consensus, i.e. groupthink.

The recent demise of scientific debate has paralleled the demise of friendly rivalry in politics as epitomised in the 1960s and 70s by the relationship between Fred Daly of the ALP and Liberal member Jim Killen in Federal Parliament. When accused of racism by Gough Whitlam, Killen said "*I, for one, swam bare-arsed in the Condamine with Aboriginals*". I haven't, but I've been inspired by Traditional Aboriginal Knowledge, especially as articulated brilliantly by Victor Steffensen.

Many stalwart whitefellas such as Barry Aitchison, Chris Commins and John Mulligan continue the fight to restore our heritage of healthy, safe and productive landscapes, following the traditional models. Without their inspiration, I'd have given up long ago.

Finally, I must especially thank all the editors, academics and bureaucrats who seem not to care for scientific debate, and have forced me to engage with what used to be known as *the man*[xxxix] *in the street*.

Note

1   Byram 1959

[xxxix]   When I was a boy, mankind was an inclusive term.

BIBLIOGRAPHY

Adams, M., Attiwill, P. 2011 *Burning issues. Sustainability and management of Australia's southern forests*. CSIRO Publishing, Collingwood.

Adams-Hosking, C., McBride, M. F., Baxter, G., Burgman, M., de Villiers, D., Kavanagh, R., Lawler, I., Lunney, D., Melzer, A., Menkhorst, P., Molsher, R., Moore, B.D., Phalen, D., Rhodes, J.R., Todd, C., Whisson, D., McAlpine, C.A. 2016 Use of expert knowledge to elicit population trends for the koala (*Phascolarctos cinereus*). *Diversity and Distributions* 22, 249-62.

AKF undated *So how many Koalas were there?* https://www.savethekoala. com/sites/savethekoala.com/files/uploads/Imagine2016FurTrade.pdf

AKF 2019 *Australian Koala Foundation calls on the new Prime Minister to protect the Koala*. Press release 10th May https://www.savethekoala. com/sites/savethekoala.com/files/uploads/AKF_press_release_10_ may_2019.pdf

Allen, C. 1995 Koalas prefer mature forests say experts. *Eden Magnet*, 23 May.

Amis, A. 2014 *Victorian Koala Issues, Plantations and Forest Stewardship Council Certification 2000–2014*. Friends of the Earth, Melbourne.

Anon. 1803 Sydney. *Sydney Gazette*, 21 August, p. 3.

Anon. 1836 On the animals called monkeys in New South Wales. Sketches of New South Wales. No. XIV. *Saturday Magazine* 288, 1-2. Committee of General Literature and Education. Society for Promoting Christian Knowledge, location unknown.

Anon. 1950 *Koala Survey* Reproduced in Reed *et al.* 1990, Appendix 1.

Anon. 2018 *Australia's State of the forests report 2018*. Criterion 1 Conservation of biological diversity. Australian Government, Department of Agriculture, ABARES.

Arentz, F. 2017 *Phytophthora cinnamomi* A1: An ancient resident of New Guinea and Australia of Gondwanan origin? *Forest Pathology*. 2017: e12342.

Arnold, S. 2017 *Koala Crisis*. The Vicious mainstream media killing koalas, Facebook 27 November 2017; *Independent Australia*. No right of reply for koalas: ABC repeats The Australian's junk science, 7 December 2017

Attiwill, P.M., Packham, D., Barker, T., Hamilton, I. 2009 *The People's Review of Bushfires, 2002-2007, in Victoria.* Final Report 2009. Richmond, Australia.

AUSLIG 1990 *Atlas of Australian Resources, Third Series, Volume 6. Vegetation.* Australian Surveying and Land Information Group, Department of Administrative Services, Canberra.

Barbones, S. 2018 The world's first immigration economy. *FP*, 3 October 2018 https://foreignpolicy.com/2018/10/03/australia-the-worlds-first-immigration-economy/

Bergin, T.J. 1978 *The Koala: proceedings of the Taronga symposium.* Zoological Parks Board of N.S.W., Sydney.

Beyer, H.L., de Villiers, D., Loader, J., Robbins, A., Stigner, M., Forbes, N., Hanger, J. 2018 Management of multiple threats achieves meaningful koala conservation outcomes. *Journal of Applied Ecology* 2018, 1-10. DOI: 10.1111/1365-2664.13127

Boer, M.M., Sadler, R.J., Wittkuhn, R.S., McCaw, L., Grierson, P.F. 2009 Long-term impacts of prescribed burning on regional extent and incidence of wildfires—evidence from 50 years of active fire management in SW Australian forests. *Forest Ecology and Management* 259, 132-42. doi: 10.1016/j.foreco.2009.10.005

Bradshaw, C.J.A., Ehrlich, P.R. 2015 *Killing the Koala and Poisoning the Prairie: Australia, America, and the Environment.* The University of Chicago Press, Chicago and London.

Brown, G., McAlpine, C., Rhodes, J., Lunney, D., Golgingay, R., Fielding, K., Hetherington, S., Hopkins, M., Manning, C., Wood, M., Brace, A., Vass, L. 2018 Assessing the validity of crowdsourced wildlife observations for conservation using public participatory mapping methods. *Biological Conservation* 227, 141-51.

Bureau of Meteorology 2019 Monthly Rainfall Poowong (Post Office) file:///D:/Users/Documents/Silviculture/koalas/Monthly%20 Rainfall%20-%20086092%20-%20Bureau%20of%20Meteorology%20 poowong.html

Burrows, N. 2016a Book review. Firestick Ecology: fairdinkum science in plain English. *International Journal of Wildland Fire* 25, 810.

Burrows, N.D. 2016b Managing Bushfire in the New Millennium. In *Bushfire 2016 Connecting Science, People & Practice.* Conference Report: Outcomes & Learnings. SEQ Fire and Biodiversity Consortium. pp. 25-32.

Burrows, N., McCaw, L. 2013 Prescribed burning in southwestern Australian forests. *Frontiers in Ecology and Environment* 11, e24-e34.

Byram, G. M. 1959 Combustion of forest fuels. In *Forest fire: control and use*. Ed. K. P. Davis. McGraw-Hill, New York. pp. 61-89.

Calaby, J.H. 1966 *Mammals of the Upper Richmond and Clarence Rivers, New South Wales*. Division of Wildlife Research Technical Paper No. 10. Commonwealth Scientific and Industrial Research Organisation, Australia.

Campbell, K.G. 1966 Aspects of insect-tree relationships in forests of eastern Australia. In *Breeding Pest-Resistant Trees. Proceedings of a N.A.T.O. and N.S.F. Symposium, Pennsylvania State University, August 30 to September 11, 1964*. Pergamon Press, New York. pp. 239-50.

Campbell, K.G., Hadlington, P. 1967 *The biology of the three species of phasmatids (Phasmatodea) which occur in plague numbers in forests of southeastern Australia*. Research Note No. 20, Forestry Commission of N.S.W., Sydney, Australia.

Carrick, F. 1990 Towards a rational debate on koala conservation issues. In *Koala Summit: managing koalas in New South Wales*. Eds. D. Lunney, C.A. Urquhart, P Reed. NSW National Parks and Wildlife Service. pp. 149-56

Carrick, F.M. 2017 Response from Professor Frank Carrick to ABC Radio National Exec. Producer Sheryle Bagwell re misleading interview relating to koala populations 04.12.2017 http://www.greatsouthernforest.org.au/media/carrick.pdf

Cheney, P. 2015 In *Fire from the sky*. Ed. R. Underwood. York Gum Publishing, Palmyra, Australia. pp. 126-7.

Clarkson, C., Jacobs, Z., Marwick, B., Fullagar, R., Wallis, L., Smith, M., Roberts, R. G., Hayes, E., Lowe, K., Carah, X. *et al*. 2017. Human occupation of northern Australia by 65,000 years ago. *Nature* 547, 306-10.

Close, R., Ward, S., Phelan, D. 2015 A dangerous idea: that Koala densities can be low without the populations being in danger. *Australian Zoologist* 38, 1-8.

Cook, D. 1993 Report attacks koala research. *Sydney Morning Herald*. Tues 13 April. p. 4.

Coverdale, T. J. 1920 The scrub. In *The Land of the Lyrebird. A Story of Early Settlement in the Great Forest of South Gippsland*. South Gippsland Pioneers' Association. Facsimile reproduction. Forgotten Books, London. pp. 31-47.

Craig, W.W., 1925 *Moreton Bay Settlement or Queensland before Separation. 1770-1859. Together with a Brief Account of the Rise of the Colonies of Australasia*. Watson, Ferguson and Co. Limited. Stanley Street, Brisbane, Queensland.

DECCW 2010 *Koala surveys in the coastal forests of the Bermagui–Mumbulla area: 2007–09. An interim report.* NSW Department of Environment, Climate Change and Water, Sydney. http://www.environment.nsw.gov.au/resources/ threatenedspecies/10116koalabermmum.pdf

DELWP 2016 *Koalas at Cape Otway.* Victoria State Government. Environment, Land, Water and Planning.

DELWP 2018 *Koala Management Plan ABP.* https://www.austgum.com. au/australian-plantations-woodchips/documents/2018-09-10-ABP_ KMP_v7_Approved20180910.pdf

Department of the Environment 2019 *Phascolarctos cinereus* (combined populations of Qld, NSW and the ACT) in *Species Profile and Threats Database*, Department of the Environment, Canberra. http://www. environment.gov.au/sprat

Dijkstra, F.A., Adams, M.A. 2015 Fire eases imbalances of nitrogen and phosphorus in woody plants. *Ecosystems* online https://link.springer. com/article/10.1007/s10021-015-9861-1

Dodd, F. 1920 Recollections and Experiences. In *The Land of the Lyrebird. A Story of Early Settlement in the Great Forest of South Gippsland.* South Gippsland Pioneers' Association. Facsimile reproduction. Forgotten Books, London. pp. 140-8.

Dye, J. 2019 Two people found dead after bushfires ravage northern NSW. *The Sydney Morning Herald* 10 October. https://www.smh. com.au/national/nsw/two-people-found-dead-after-bushfire-ravages-nsw-town-20191010-p52zj8.html

Ellis, S., Kanowski, P., Whelan, R. 2004 *National Inquiry on Bushfire Mitigation and Management.* Council of Australian Governments, Canberra.

Ellis, W., Melzer, A., Clifton, I. D., Carrick, F. 2010 Climate change and the koala *Phascolarctos cinereus*: water and energy. *Australian Zoologist* 35, 369-77. Doi:10.7882/AZ.2010.025

Elms, A.W., 1920. The early history of Westernport. In *The Land of the Lyrebird. A Story of Early Settlement in the Great Forest of South Gippsland.* South Gippsland Pioneers' Association. Facsimile reproduction. Forgotten Books, London. pp. 18-27.

Evans, L., Lane, J., Turnbull, T. 2019 *Could koalas become extinct by 2050 or are koala populations rising?* AAP FactCheck 19 March. https://factcheck.aap.com.au/claims/could-koalas-become-extinct-by-2050-or-are-koala-populations-rising

Farr, J.D., Swain, D., Metcalf, F. 2004 Spatial analysis of an outbreak of *Uraba lugens* (Lepidoptera: Noctuidae) in the south-west of Western Australia: does logging, vegetation type or fire influence outbreaks? *Australian Forestry* 67, 101-13.

Field, B. 1825 *Geographical Memoirs on New South Wales*. John Murray, London, England.

Flood, J. 2006 *The Original Australians: story of the Aboriginal people*. Allen & Unwin, Sydney.

Forbes, T., O'Brien, C. 2018 *Nearly half of Coomera koalas die after Gold Coast relocation*. ABC News 2 August 2018, Sydney. https://www.abc.net.au/news/2018-08-02/koalas-die-at-new-gold-coast-location/10065004

Ford, F. 2014 *John Gould's Extinct & Endangered Mammals of Australia*. NLA Publishing, Canberra.

Forestry Corporation and OEH 2017 *Murrah Flora Reserves Draft Final Working Plan*. NSW Government.

Gammage, B. 2011 *The biggest estate on earth: how Aborigines made Australia*. Allen & Unwin, Sydney.

Gonzalez-Astudillo, V., Allavena, R., McKinnon, A., Larkin, R., Henning, J. 2017 Decline causes of koalas in south east Queensland, Australia: a 17-year retrospective study of mortality and morbidity. *Scientific Reports* 7, 1–10. doi:10.1038/srep42587

Gordon, G., Hrdina, F. 2005 Koala and possum populations in Queensland during the harvest period 1906-1936. *Australian Zoologist* 33, 69-99.

Gordon, G., Hrdina, F., Patterson, R. 2006 Decline in the distribution of the Koala *Phascolarctos cinereus* in Queensland. *Australian Zoologist* 33, 345-58

Gould, J. 1863 *The Mammals of Australia*. John Gould, London.

Griffith, J.E., Dhand, N.K., Krockenberger, M.K., Higgins, D.P. 2013 Admission trends of koalas to a rehabilitation facility over 30 years. *Journal of Wildlife Diseases* 49, 18-28

Grogan, L.F., Peel, A.J., Kerlin, D., Ellis, W., Jones, D., Hero, J.-M., McCallum, H. 2018 Is disease a major causal factor in declines? An Evidence Framework and case study on koala chlamydiosis. *Biological Conservation* 221, 334-44.

Hannam, P. 2018 Tathra losses unlikely to have been worsened by lack of planned burns. *Sydney Morning Herald* 20 March.

Hodgson, A. 1968 Control burning in eucalypt forests in Victoria, Australia. *Journal of Forestry* 66, 601-5

Holmes, W. H.C. 1920 Scrub Cutting. In *The Land of the Lyrebird. A Story of Early Settlement in the Great Forest of South Gippsland.* South Gippsland Pioneers' Association. Facsimile reproduction. Forgotten Books, London. pp. 67-78.

Hopkins, P. 2019 Former fire chief calls for research. *Latrobe Valley Express* 11 April.

Horton, B.M. 2012 Mitigating the effects of forest eucalypt dieback associated with psyllids and bell miners in World Heritage Areas. *Australasian Plant Conservation* 20, 11-3.

House of Representatives Select Committee 2003 *A Nation Charred: Inquiry into the Recent Australian Bushfires.* Parliament of the Commonwealth of Australia, Canberra.

Howitt, A.W. 1891 The eucalypts of Gippsland. *Transactions of the Royal Society of Victoria* II, 81-120.

Howitt A.W. 1904 *The Native Tribes of South-East Australia.* Macmillan and Co. Ltd., London

Insurance News 2019 *Saving koalas: insurer launches campaign.* 13 August.

Iredale, T., Whitley, G. 1934 The early history of the koala. *Victorian Naturalist* LI, 62-72.

Jurskis, V. 2002 Separating cause and effect: koala overbrowsing as a symptom of eucalypt dieback. In *How the past affects the koala's future, proceedings from the conference on the status of the koala in 2002.* Australian Koala Foundation, Brisbane.

Jurskis, V. 2005 Eucalypt decline in Australia, and a general concept of tree decline and dieback. *Forest Ecology and Management* 215, 1-20.

Jurskis, V. 2011a Benchmarks of fallen timber and man's role in nature: some evidence from temperate eucalypt woodlands in southeastern Australia. *Forest Ecology and Management* 261, 2149-56.

Jurskis, V. 2011b Human fire maintains a balance of nature. In *Proceedings of Bushfire CRC & AFAC 2011 Conference Science Day, 1 September 2011, Sydney, Australia.* Ed. R.P. Thorton   Bushfire Cooperative Research Centre, Melbourne, Australia. pp. 129-38.

Jurskis, V. 2015 *Firestick Ecology: Fairdinkum Science in Plain English.* Connor Court Pty Ltd.

Jurskis, V. 2017a Ecological history of the koala and implications for management. *Wildlife Research* 44, 471-83. doi.org/10.1071/WR17032

Jurskis, V. 2017b Mooted extinction of koalas at Eden: improving the information base. *Wildlife Research* 44, 449-52. doi.org/10.1071/ WR16171

Jurskis, V., Potter M. 1997 *Koala Surveys, Ecology and Conservation at Eden.* Research Paper No. 34. State Forests of New South Wales, Sydney.

Jurskis, V., Turner, J. 2002. Eucalypt dieback in eastern Australia: a simple model. *Australian Forestry* 65, 81-92.

Jurskis, V., Underwood, R. 2013 Human fires and wildfires on Sydney sandstones: History informs fire management. *Fire Ecology* 9, 8-24.

Jurskis, V., Walmsley, T. 2011 Eucalypt ecosystems predisposed to chronic decline: estimated distribution in coastal New South Wales. Bushfire Cooperative Research Centre, Melbourne, Australia. Available online: http://www.bushfirecrc.com/publications/biblio/ag/ J?sort=author&order=desc

Jurskis, V., Douch, A., McCray, K., Shields, J. 2001 A playback survey of the koala, *Phascolarctos cinereus*, and a review of its distribution in the Eden region of south-eastern New South Wales. *Australian Forestry* 64, 226-31. doi:10.1080/00049158.2001.10676193

Jurskis, V., Bridges, B., de Mar, P. 2003 Fire management in Australia: the lessons of 200 years. In *Joint Australia and New Zealand Institute of Forestry Conference Proceedings, 27 April–1 May 2003, Queenstown, New Zealand.* Eds. E.G. Mason, C.J. Perley. Ministry of Agriculture and Forestry, Wellington, New Zealand, pp. 353-68.

Jurskis, V., de Mar, P., Aitchison, B. 2006 Fire management in the alpine region. In *Bushfire 2006. Life in a fire prone environment: translating science into practice.* Ed C. Tran. Griffith University, Brisbane, Australia. CD.

Jurskis, V., Turner, J., Lambert, M., Bi, H. 2011 Fire and N cycling: getting the perspective right. *Applied Vegetation Science* 14, 433-4. doi:10.1111/ j.1654-109X.2011.01130.x

Kavanagh, R. P., Debus, S., Tweedie, T., Webster, R. 1995 Distribution of nocturnal forest birds and mammals in north-eastern New South Wales: relationships with environmental variables and management history. *Wildlife Research* 22, 359-77. doi:10.1071/WR9950359

Kershaw, J. A. 1934 The koala on Wilson's Promontory. *Victorian Naturalist* LI, 76-7.

Kjeldsen, S.R., Zenger, K.R., Leigh, K., Ellis, W., Tobey, J., Phalen, D., Melzer, A., FitzGibbon, S., Raadsma, H.W., 2016 Genome-wide SNP loci reveal novel insights into koala (*Phascolarctos cinereus*) population variability across its range. *Conservation Genetics* 17, 337-53.

Laurance, W.F., Useche, D.C., Rendeiro, J. *et al.* 2012 Averting biodiversity collapse in tropical forest protected areas. *Nature* 489, 290-3.

Law, B.S., Brassil, T., Gonsalves, L., Roe, P., Truskinger, A., McConville, A. 2018 Passive acoustics and sound recognition provide new insights on status and resilience of an iconic endangered marsupial (koala *Phascolarctos cinereus*) to timber harvesting. *PLoS ONE* 13: e0205075. https://doi.org/10.1371/journal.pone.0205075

Law, B., Gonsalves, L., Bilney, R., Peterie, J., Pietsch, R., Roe, P., Truskinger, A. 2019 Using passive acoustic recording and automated call identification to survey koalas in the southern forests of New South Wales. *Australian Zoologist.* DOI: https://doi.org/10.7882/AZ.2019.033

Lee, A., Martin, R. 1988 *The Koala: A Natural History*. New South Wales University Press, Sydney.

Lee, A.K., Martin, R.W., Handasyde, K.A. 1990 Experimental translocation of koalas to new habitat. In *Biology of the Koala*. Eds. A. K. Lee, K. A. Handasyde, G. D. Sanson. Surrey Beatty, Sydney. pp. 299-312.

Lewis, F. 1934 The koala in Victoria. *Victorian Naturalist* LI, 73-6.

Luke, R.H., McArthur, A.G. 1978 *Bushfires in Australia*. AGPS Canberra.

Lunney, D. 2019 Testimony in *Report of Proceedings Before Portfolio Committee No. 7 – Planning and Environment: Inquiry into Koala Populations and Habitat in New South Wales. At Macquarie Room, Parliament House, Sydney on Monday 9 December 2019.*

Lunney, D., Barker, J. 1986/7 Mammals of the coastal forests near Bega, New South Wales. *Australian Zoologist* 23, 19-28; 41-9.

Lunney D., Leary T. 1988 The impact on native mammals of land-use changes and exotic species in the Bega district, New South Wales, since settlement. *Australian Journal of Ecology* 13, 67-92.

Lunney, D., Esson, C., Moon, C., Ellis, M., Matthews, A. 1997 A community-based survey of the koala, *Phascolarctos cinereus*, in the Eden region of south-eastern New South Wales. *Wildlife Research* 24, 111-28. doi:10.1071/WR94034

Lunney, D., Crowther, M. S., Shannon, I., Bryant, J. V. 2009 Combining a map-based public survey with an estimation of site occupancy to determine the recent and changing distribution of the koala in New South Wales. *Wildlife Research* 36, 262-73. doi:10.1071/WR08079

Lunney, D., Close, R., Bryant, J., Crowther, M. S., Shannon, I., Madden, K., Ward, S. 2010 Campbelltown's koalas: their place in the natural history of

Sydney. In *The Natural History of Sydney*. Eds. D. Lunney, P. Hutchings and D. Hochuli. Royal Zoological Society of NSW, Sydney. pp. 319-25.

Lunney, D., Stalenberg, E., Santika, T., Rhodes, J. R. 2014 Extinction in Eden: identifying the role of climate change in the decline of the koala in south-eastern NSW. *Wildlife Research* 41, 22-34. doi:10.1071/WR13054

Lunney, D., Wells, A., Miller, I. 2016a An Ecological History of the Koala *Phascolarctos cinereus* in Coffs Harbour and its Environs, on the Mid-north Coast of New South Wales, c1861-2000 *Proceedings of the Linnean Society of New South Wales* 138, 1-48

Lunney, D., Predavec, M., Miller, I., Shannon, I., Fisher, M., Moon, C., Matthews, A., Turbill, J., Rhodes, J. R. 2016b Interpreting patterns of population change in koalas from longterm datasets in Coffs Harbour on the north coast of New South Wales. *Australian Mammalogy* 38, 29-43. doi:10.1071/AM15019

Lunney, D., Stalenberg, E., Santika, T., Rhodes, J. R. 2017a A rebuttal to 'Mooted extinction of koalas at Eden: improving the information base' *Wildlife Research* 44, 453-57

Lunney, D., Predavec, M., Sonawane, I., Kavanagh, R., Barrott-Brown, G., Phillips, S., Callaghan, J., Mitchell, D., Parnaby, H., Paull, D.C., Shannon, I., Ellis, M., Price, O., Milledge, D., 2017b The remaining koalas (*Phascolarctos cinereus*) of the Pilliga forests, north-west New South Wales: refugial persistence or a population on the road to extinction? *Pacific Conservation Biology* 23, 277-94. doi.org/10.1071/PC17008

MacKenzie, C. 1934 Comparative anatomy and the koala. *Victorian Naturalist* LI, 58-61.

MacNally, R., Cunningham, S.C., Baker, P.J., Horner, G.J., Thomson, J.R. 2011 Dynamics of Murray-Darling floodplain forests under multiple stressors: The past, present, and future of an Australian icon. *Water Resources Research* 47, W00G05 doi:10.1029/2011WR010383

Marshall, A.J. 1966 Ed. *The Great Extermination: A guide to Anglo-Australian cupidity wickedness & waste*. Heinemann.

McAlpine, C., Lunney, D., Melzer, A., Menkhorst, P., Phillips, S., Phalen, D., Ellis, W., Foley, W., Baxter, G., de Villiers, D., Kavanagh, R., Adams-Hosking, C., Todd, C., Whisson, D., Molsher, R., Walter, M., Lawler, I., Close, R. 2015 Conserving koalas: a review of the contrasting regional trends, outlooks and policy challenges. *Biological Conservation* 192, 226-36. doi:10.1016/j.biocon.2015.09.020

McCaw, L. 2016 Book Review. Firestick Ecology: fairdinkum science in plain English. *Fire Ecology* 12, 124-5.

Melzer, A., Carrick, F., Menkhorst, P., Lunney, D., St. John, B. 2000 Overview, critical assessment, and conservation implications of koala distribution and abundance. *Conservation Biology* 14, 619-28. doi:10.1046/j.1523-1739.2000.99383.x

Melzer, A., Lamb, D. 1994 Low density populations of the Koala *(Phascolarctos cinereus)* in Central Queensland. *Proceedings of the Royal Society of Queensland* 104, 89-93.

Menkhorst, P. 2008 Hunted, marooned, re-introduced, contracepted: a history of Koala management in Victoria. In *Too Close for Comfort: Contentious Issues in Human–wildlife Encounters*. Eds. D. Lunney, A. Munn, W. Meikle. Royal Zoological Society of New South Wales, Sydney. pp. 73-92.

Menkhorst, P., Ramsey, D., O'Brien, T., Hynes, E., Whisson, D. 2019 Survival and movements of koalas translocated from an over-abundant population. *Wildlife Research* 46, 557-65.

Mitchell, T.L. 1848 *Journal of an Expedition into the Interior of Tropical Australia in Search of a Route from Sydney to the Gulf of Carpentaria*. Longman, Brown, Green and Longmans, London. Facsimile Edition 2007. Archive CD Books, Australia.

Mooney, S.D., Harrison, S.P., Bartlein, P.J., Daniau, A.-L., Stevenson, J., Brownlie, K.C., Buckman, S., Cupper, M., Luly, J., Black, M., Colhoun, E., D'Costa, D., Dodson, J., Haberle, S., Hope, G.S., Kershaw, P., Kenyon, C., McKenzie, M., Williams, N. 2011 Late quaternary fire regimes of Australia. *Quaternary Science Reviews* 30, 28-46.

Moore, K.M. 1961 Observations on some Australian forest insects 8. The biology and occurrence of *Glycaspis baileyi* Moore in New South Wales. *Proceedings of the Linnean Society of New South Wales* 86, 185-200.

Moore, B., Whisson, D. 2015 Victorian koalas are eating themselves out of house and home. *The Conversation* 11 March. https://theconversation.com/victorian-koalas-are-eating-themselves-out-of-house-and-home-38585

Morton, N. 2019 Busbys Flat bushfire, Fire and Rescue NSW lend a helping hand. *Western Advocate* 15 October. https://www.westernadvocate.com.au/story/6439565/see-the-fire-ravaged-town-that-bathurst-and-kelso-firefighters-helped/

Museum of Applied Arts and Sciences 2018 Road sign 'Koala' https://collection.maas.museum/object/398246

NPA 2019 *The Great Koala National Park* https://npansw.org/npa/campaigns/

great-koala-national-park/

NRC 2019a *Research Program Plan: Koala response to regeneration harvesting in North Coast state forests.* NSW Government.

NRC 2019b *DRAFT Coastal Integrated Forestry Approvals Monitoring Program 2019-2024.* For public review. NSW Government.

NRC 2019c *Supporting post-fire ecological resilience and recovery planning in NSW forests. Forest Monitoring and Improvement Program - Foundational Project.* Project Overview. NSW Government.

NSW Government 1996 *Forestry Revocation and National Park Reservation Act 1996 No. 131*

NSW Government 2018 $4 million for new bushfire research hub. https://www.environment.nsw.gov.au/news/four-million-dollars-for-new-bushfire-research-hub

OEH 2016 *2012–14 Koala survey report in coastal forests of south-eastern NSW – Bermagui/Mumbulla area.* Office of Environment and Heritage, Sydney.

OEH 2018a *Developing a whole-of-government NSW Koala Strategy. Public engagement summary report.* NSW Government.

OEH 2018b *NSW Koala Strategy.* NSW Government.

O'Kane, M. 2016 *Report of the independent review into the decline of koala populations in key areas of NSW.* NSW Chief Scientist and Engineer, Sydney.

Parris, H. S. 1948 Koalas on the lower Goulburn. *Victorian Naturalist* 64, 192-3.

Penman, T.D., Christie, F.J., Andersen, A.N., Bradstock, R.A., Cary, G.J., Henderson, M.K., Price, O., Tran, C., Wardle, G.M., Williams, R.J., York, A. 2011 Prescribed burning: how can it work to conserve the things we value? *International Journal of Wildland Fire* 20, 721-33.

Phillips, B. 1990 *Koalas: The little Australians we'd all hate to lose.* AGPS Press, Canberra

Predavec, M. 2016 NSW Koala Population Case Studies. Office of NSW Chief Scientist and Engineer, Sydney? http://www.chiefscientist.nsw.gov.au/__data/assets/pdf_file/0003/94521/Koala-population-case-studies.pdf

Price, O.F., Penman, T.D., Bradstock, R.A., Boer, M.M., Clarke, H. 2015 Biogeographical variation in the potential effectiveness of prescribed fire in south-eastern Australia. *Journal of Biogeography.* Available online: http://wileyonlinelibrary.com/journal/jbi doi:10.1111/jbi.12579

Pringle, R.M., Syfert, M., Webb, J.K., Shine, R. 2009 Quantifying historical changes in habitat availability for endangered species: use of pixel- and object-based remote sensing. *Journal of Applied Ecology* 46, 544-53.

Ransome, A. 1947 *Great Northern?* Jonathan Cape

Reed, P., Lunney, D. 1990 Habitat loss: the key problem for the long term survival of koalas in NSW. In *Koala Summit: managing koalas in New South Wales.* Eds. D. Lunney, C.A. Urquhart, P Reed. NSW National Parks and Wildlife Service. pp. 9-31.

Reed, P., Lunney, D., Walker, P. 1990 A 1986–1987 survey of the koala *Phascolarctos cinereus* (Goldfuss) in New South Wales and an ecological interpretation of its distribution. In *Biology of the Koala.* Eds. A. K. Lee, K. A. Handasyde, G. D. Sanson. Surrey Beatty, Sydney. pp. 55-74.

Rennison, B. 2017 *Bioregional assessment of koala populations in NSW.* A report prepared for the Office of Environment and Heritage. Released under GIPA1026

RFS 2006 *Bush Fire Environmental Assessment Code for New South Wales.* NSW Rural Fire Service.

Roberts, S. 2016 Koala Park Sanctuary fined $75,000 *The Daily Telegraph* 3 February. https://www.dailytelegraph.com.au/newslocal/the-hills/koala-park-sanctuary-fined-75000/news-story/1a25697c8ee77b9dc8e4636bcc0cc9e9

Robinson, A.C. 1978 The koala in South Australia. In *The Koala. Proceedings of the Taronga Symposium.* Ed T.J. Bergin. Zoological Parks Board of N.S.W. pp. 132-43.

Rolls, E. 1981 *A Million Wild Acres.* Thirtieth Anniversary Edition, 2011. Hale & Iremonger, McMahon's Point.

San Diego Zoo 2019 Koala (*Phascolarctos cinereus*) Fact Sheet: Population & Conservation Status http://ielc.libguides.com/sdzg/factsheets/koala/population

Silver, M.J., Carnegie A.J. 2017 *An independent review of bell miner associated dieback.* Final report prepared for the Project Steering Committee: systematic review of bell miner associated dieback. Office of Environment and Heritage, Sydney.

Smith, H., Ximenes, F. 2019 *Production Forest Methodologies for the Emissions Reduction Fund.* Forest and Wood Products Australia, Melbourne.

Sneeuwjagt, R.J. 2008 Prescribed burning: how effective is it in the control of large bushfires? In *Fire, Environment and society: From Research to Practice.* Bushfire Co-operative Research Centre and Australian Fire

Authorities Council, Adelaide, Australia, pp. 419-35.

South Eastern Australian Climate Initiative, 2011. *The Millenium Drought and 2010/2011 Floods.* CSIRO July 2011. http://www.seaci.org/publications/documents/SEACI-2Reports/SEACI2_Factsheet2of4_WEB_110714.pdf Accessed 8/08/2018.

Speakman, M., Blair, N. 2016 *NSW Government Protects South Coast Koalas and Local Timber Industry.* Media Release Tuesday, 1 March 2016

Stalenberg, E., Wallis, I. R., Cunningham, R. B., Allen, C., Foley, W. J. 2014. Nutritional correlates of koala persistence in a low-density population. *PLoS One* 9, e113930. doi:10.1371/journal.pone.0113930

Stanton, P., Stanton, D., Stott, M., Parsons, M. 2014 Fire exclusion and the changing landscape of Queensland's Wet Tropics Bioregion. *Australian Forestry* 77, 51-68.

State Forests of NSW 1995 *Urbenville Management Area: proposed forestry operations. Environmental Impact Statement.* State Forests of New South Wales, Pennant Hills.

Steele, J.G. 1984 *Aboriginal pathways: in Southeast Queensland and the Richmond River.* University of Queensland Press.

Steffensen, V. 2019 Testimony. In *Report of Proceedings Before Portfolio Committee No. 7 – Planning and Environment: Inquiry into Koala Populations and Habitat in New South Wales.* At Macquarie Room, Parliament House, Sydney on Monday 9 December 2019. pp. 22-9

Strzelecki, P.E. 1845 *Physical Description of New South Wales and Van Die-man's Land, accompanied by a Geological Map, Sections and Diagrams, and Figures of the organic remains.* Google Books. https://play.google.com/books/eader?id=ftUKAAAAIAAJ&printsec=frontcover&output=reader&hl=en&pg=GBS.PR1

Tabart, D. 2019 *Koala myth becomes scientific fact.* Australian Koala Foundation, Brisbane. https://www.savethekoala.com/sites/savethekoala.com/files/uploads/koalamythbecomesscientificfact.pdf

The Senate. Environment and Communication References Committee 2011 *The koala – saving our national icon.* Commonwealth of Australia.

The Senate. Environment and Communication References Committee 2019 *Australia's faunal extinction crisis. Interim Report.* Commonwealth of Australia.

Tilley, D., Uebel, K. 1990 Observations of koala populations within the Sydney Water Board's Upper Nepean catchment area. In *Koala Summit: managing koalas in New South Wales.* Eds. D. Lunney, C.A. Urquhart, P Reed. NSW National Parks and Wildlife Service. pp. 81-4.

Turner, J., Lambert, M., Jurskis, V., Bi, H. 2008 Long term accumulation of nitrogen in soils of dry mixed eucalypt forest in the absence of fire. *Forest Ecology and Management* 256, 1133-42.

Underwood, R. 2013 *Foresters of the Raj.* York Gum Publishing, Australia.

Underwood, R. 2015 *Fire from the Sky.* York Gum Publishing, Australia.

University of Western Sydney 2013 *Bugs that ate a fragile woodland.* Research Directions. NSW Government, NSW Environmental Trust http://www.uws.edu.au/__data/assets/pdf_file/0010/582166/Riegler_grey_box_dieback_FINAL_with_image.pdf

University of Western Sydney 2019 *EucFACE* https://www.westernsydney.edu.au/hie/EucFACE

van Kempen, E. 1997 *A History of the Pilliga Cypress Pine Forests.* State Forests of New South Wales, Pennant Hills.

Wall, D. 1933 *Blinky Bill: The Quaint Little Australian.* Read Books Ltd. 2011 Edition.

Wedrowicz, F., Wright, W., Schlagloth, R., Santamaria, F., Cahir, F. 2017 Landscape, koalas and people: A historical account of koala populations and their environment in South Gippsland. *Australian Zoologist* 38, 518-36

Wesson, S. 2000 *An Historical Atlas of the Aborigines of Eastern Victoria and far South-eastern New South Wales.* Monash Publications in Geography and Environmental Science. Number 53. School of Geography and Environmental Science: Monash University, Melbourne.

Whisson, D.A., Holland, G.J., Carlyon, K. 2012 Translocation of overabundant species: Implications for translocated individuals. *Journal of Wildlife Management* 76, 1661-9

Whisson, D.A., Dixon, V., Taylor, M.L., Melzer, A. 2016. Failure to respond to food resource decline has catastrophic consequences for koalas in a high-density population in southern Australia. *Plos One* 11, 1-12. doi:10.1371/journal.pone.0144348

White, N. A., Kunst, N. D. 1990 Aspects of the ecology of the koala in south-eastern Queensland. In *Biology of the Koala.* Eds. A. K. Lee, K. A. Handasyde, G. D. Sanson. Surrey Beatty, Sydney. pp. 109-66.

Wikipedia 2019 *Strzelecki Ranges* https://en.wikipedia.org/wiki/Strzelecki_Ranges

WWF 2018a *NSW Koala Strategy "ineffective inadequate and expensive"* https://www.wwf.org.au/news/news/2018/nsw-koala-strategy-ineffective-inadequate-and-expensive#gs.6nagia

WWF 2018b Koala Extinction Risk NSW file:///C:/Users/Vic%20Jurskis/Downloads/pub-Koala-extinction-risk-NSW-28sept18%20(5).pdf

WWF 2019 Koala Habitat Conservation Plan. WWF-Australia file:///C:/Users/Vic%20Jurskis/Downloads/WWF-Koala%20Habitat%20Conservation%20Plan-Abridged%20(2).pdf

Zhang, Z., Peterson, J., Zhu, X., Wright, W. 2008 Long Term Land use and land cover change and its impact on cool temperate rainforest in the Strzelecki Ranges, Australia. *The International Archives of the Photogrammetry, Remote Sensing and Spatial Information Sciences.* Vol. XXXVII. Part B7. Beijing 2008. pp. 899-904

www.ingramcontent.com/pod-product-compliance
Lightning Source LLC
Chambersburg PA
CBHW070348270326
41926CB00017B/4034